sent
to
soar

sent
to
soar

FULFILL YOUR
DIVINE POTENTIAL
FOR YOURSELF AND
FOR THE WORLD

REV. STEPHEN POOS-BENSON

QUEST
BOOKS

Theosophical Publishing House
Wheaton, Illinois * Chennai, India

Quest Books
Theosophical Publishing House
PO Box 270
Wheaton, Illinois 60187-0270

www.questbooks.net

Cover image © iStock.com/leisuretime70
Cover design by Drew Stevens
Typesetting by Wordstop, Chennai, India

Library of Congress Cataloging-in-Publication Data

Poos-Benson, Stephen.
Sent to soar: fulfill your divine potential for yourself and for the world /
Rev. Stephen Poos-Benson.—First Quest edition.
        pages   cm
Includes bibliographical references and index.
ISBN 978-0-8356-0922-7
1. Spiritual life.   2. Religions.   I. Title.
BL624.P645 2014
204'.4—dc23   2014001201

5 4 3 2 1 * 14 15 16 17 18 19 20

Printed in the United States of America

To the four who soar beside me—
Phoebe, Kyle, Kelsey, and Taylor.

Table of Contents

TABLE OF CONTENTS

TABLE OF CONTENTS

TABLE OF CONTENTS

Preface

It's an era of pink slips. No one is exempt. Engineers, doctors, attorneys, teachers, firefighters, garbage collectors—all sorts of people are getting pink slips in almost every line of work.

In the congregation that I serve, many have been handed the dreaded pink slip. Consequently, they've lost their homes, their cars, and their dignity. In our neighborhoods, on almost every block, there are front lawns stacked with beds and dressers with bras and underwear hanging out, jackets and pants heaped in piles, the intimacies of people's lives laid bare for the world to see. These are the signs of eviction and the signs of the times.

People are scrambling for work. Any job will do as they fight for the basic necessities of life—a roof over their heads, food on the table, and clothes on their back. Professional people who had careers, 401Ks, and pensions and who once bought groceries for our church's food banks now go to such food banks themselves to feed their kids. Our suburban Denver neighborhoods are just like countless neighborhoods all across the United States. People are facing economic challenges unlike anything they have seen before.

Throw into the mix the usual crises that occur in people's lives—cancer, strokes, diabetes, death, wars, conflicts around the world—and it's clear that we are living in some fairly harsh times. Sure, there have been harder eras. The elder members of our church say that what we are going through is nothing compared to the Great

Depression, when unemployment was easily twice what it is now. It wasn't just the occasional neighbors who lost homes, but whole neighborhoods of people. Entire towns disappeared in the economic crash. When our elders think of hard times, they describe Flanders Fields and the trench warfare of WWI. They speak of the beaches of Normandy, the Holocaust, the razing of Warsaw, and the bombings of Hiroshima and Nagasaki. Every era of humanity has been wracked by pain, agony, and death. So what we're going through isn't new. What makes it especially significant to us is that now *we're the ones going through it.* These are *our* hard times.

In the midst of our troubled times, I feel called to write a book based on hope. While life feels particularly scattered about, if not downright tragic, the hope is that God's purpose, a divine holy presence, is working its way through human history. I believe the Creator has sent *us* into the world at this specific time to accomplish something grand. There is intention behind this action. Each of us has a role to play in stitching together the next phase of human evolution.

This Being has sent people throughout the ages. I believe it has sent each human life at particular moments to fulfill a divine dream. The challenge, though, is that since we are living now, we must discern why the Creator has sent *us*. Each of us must ask and answer, "What is my role? What am I supposed to do? What is there about my life that brings a unique shape to the world?" I believe that, given this challenge, people must discover their reason for being. *Sent to Soar* is different from other books that talk about receiving a calling for a vocation. This book contends that while discovering meaning through a vocation is important, what is significant is that we have been sent to live now. We've been given gifts for a reason, and we need to discover and hone them to perfection. We need to discern our life's purpose and to live it as large as we can. As individuals, we bring our gifts to the forefront of our lives. As groups—businesses, towns, social groups, churches, schools, colleges, web groups—we collaborate, and the Creator collaborates with us. The calling for us as individuals and as groups is to discern why we have been sent at this time into the world, and then to work to fulfill this dream.

I don't know what has happened to you. I don't know your life circumstances. But whatever they are, I know that you have been sent here. I hope to capture your imagination. I want to inspire you to wonder why you are here and to challenge you to fulfill a divine dream.

While I write this book to you as an individual, I'm hoping that this "you" will become collective. While the Creator sends and works with individuals, it also brings groups of people together to collaborate. As individuals discover why they've been sent, and work together, a great synergy will be released that significantly impacts *our* era. I pray that *Sent to Soar* may be a spark for that conversation.

You are here to enable the divine purpose of the
universe to unfold.

—Eckhart Tolle

Introduction

Have you ever felt that you were *supposed* to be doing something more with your life? That little niggling in your being that creates this sense of *"supposed to"* implies intention. If you are *supposed* to be doing something, then something, or someone, has planted that notion within you.

Now, it could be argued that a parent, teacher, or mentor planted the thought of *supposed to*, but I would disagree. While these people shape many of our desires and interests, I believe that this sense of *"supposed to"* has a divine origin.

Before your conception, God, a great cosmic entity, held the luminescence of your soul, planted a certain set of destinies within it, and endowed it with gifts to fulfill a divine dream. This "dream" became you. The Creator sent you into the world and your life journey began. This uncanny sense that you're *supposed to* be doing something with your life is a hint of a divine dream for you. Unless you devote yourself to discerning what you are *supposed to* be doing, you will feel unfinished and incomplete. Conversely, you will experience ultimate joy when you have discovered your divine destiny and you are living it to its fullest. Throughout this book I'm going to push on that tension of what you're *supposed to* be doing. And beyond just pushing, I intend to empower you to discover this divine dream.

INTRODUCTION

Sent to Soar is based upon a few key assumptions that I make about the Creator, creation, and life.

My first assumption is that a divine entity exists. This may sound obvious, but it needs to be stated. However, I also know that there are as many different concepts of this holy entity as there are people on the planet. It is called by a vast array of names: Yahweh, God, Allah, Brahman, Tao, HaShem, and Wakan Tanka, to name a few. I am not going to assume that you and I have the same idea of who this divine presence is, what it looks like, or what to call it. What is important, though, is that you have a concept of a higher power, a cosmic being that is active in the world. I assume that you have faith in this entity and that it is the author of creation. I have a deep respect for all world religions and the names by which they call upon the Divine Being. I struggled to find the right term to use when referring to the Deity. I have chosen to move back and forth between the terms *Creator*, *Cosmic Being*, *Ultimate Being*, and *God*. When I refer to a particular religion I use the appropriate term for that faith: *Brahman* for Hinduism, *God* for Christianity, *HaShem* for Judaism, the *Tao* for Taoism, and *Allah* for Islam.

While there is always a risk of offending someone, I hope to find common ground where all readers may identify their own traditions. Also, I understand that each faith tradition contains a wide spectrum of beliefs. After listening for thirty years to various Christians, Buddhists, and Hindus, I clearly realize that we have major disagreements even within our own faiths. There is not a single "Christian" perspective on any given topic. The same is true for Hinduism, Buddhism, Islam, Judaism, and Taoism. While some find the diversity disconcerting, I find it enlightening. As you read this book, I ask you to be mindful of this vast spectrum and to be open to new ideas and concepts.

2

My goal is to present each of these faiths from a neutral perspective. I don't believe one religion owns the corner on the market of truth—each has many truths to share. Nor do I believe in the popular notion that all religions ultimately say the same thing. They are vastly different; yet, their spiritual insights weave a beautiful tapestry in which they enrich one another. We need each of the world's religions to gain the whole perspective on who the Creator is and what is going on in the divine consciousness. I hope that by reading this book, you'll be more inclined to pick up a book of sacred scriptures other than your own and maybe even attend a different place to worship.

My second assumption in this book is that the Creator is deeply embedded in creation and is very active in the world as it evolves. I believe that the Creator's original intention for the universe impregnates every moment of existence. Every thought, every breath, is filled with holy purpose.

My third assumption is that a divine intention is embedded within you and that you yourself have been sent into creation. I am not going to assume that you agree with me on this point; instead, I hope to wake you up to this notion. I'm going to push, prod, light firecrackers, jolt you from your sleep, and poke fingers in your soul. I'm going to use teachings from Christianity, Judaism, Hinduism, Taoism, and Buddhism, reasoning, and stories from people's lives to convince you that you, just as you are now, have been *sent*.

I know this premise raises some serious questions. Does the Creator really work this way? Does it actually send people into the world with a holy purpose? Initially, you may feel bombarded with such ideas, but with each succeeding chapter it should become more clear that, indeed, this is the case. You are here for a reason. The Creator has sent you.

INTRODUCTION

In chapter 1, I argue that part of the nature of the Ultimate Being is to intentionally send people into the creation. In chapter 2, I argue that it works within us as a driving force. Chapter 3 discusses the sticky issue of free will—as either the greatest bane or the greatest blessing upon our existence. Chapter 4 asserts that, more than just having a plan the Creator has specific plans for *us*—plural. Chapter 5 works out the nitty-gritty of how to discern your holy purpose. Chapters 6 and 7 wrestle with questions of suffering and evil. In chapter 8, I contend that we are not sent alone. To fulfill our destiny, we need to learn how to collaborate with others. Chapter 9 tells the story of a time when a tragedy crashed into my own life in the massacre at Columbine High School in 1999. That painful day was the antecedent for almost everything I've written. What I teach here are not just theories. They are techniques I have used, not only to help other people rebuild their lives, but—and maybe more important—to help myself. Chapter 10 encourages you to engage the destiny for which you have been sent. It presents the many challenges confronting you if you are to bring to fruition your purpose in being sent into the world.

There are concrete steps you can take to discern the dream that the Divine Presence has for you. The questions at the end of each chapter walk you through these steps. By responding to the questions, you'll be able to come to your own conclusions. As you finish each chapter, I encourage you write out your responses. If you are reading this book as part of a group study, these questions are a great way to start a conversation. While I assume you won't agree with everything I say, I hope to inspire a discussion that leads you to draw your own conclusions for your life's purpose.

Sent to Soar includes life stories of people sharing the ways they discovered their divine destinies and how they live them each day.

Many names and some identifying features have been changed, and in some instances people or situations are composites.

I believe I have been sent by the Creator to wake you up. You are here for a reason. I pray that by the book's end you will know in your core essence that you have been sent here for something grand. May you enjoy the process of discovery and the deep meaning that comes from dedicating your life to unleashing your divine destiny.

It is your obligation to speak things that have truth, because this is your life's work.

—Judith Black

My Story

I have had two seminal experiences in which the Creator revealed to me that I was sent: I was visited by Jesus and by Lakshmi.

I was eighteen years old, a freshman in college. I had gotten in late from a night of partying off-campus at my small Christian college in Spokane, Washington. It's not that I was a heavy drinker; it was just that I was free. Freshman year was liberating! Those first six months I felt as though I had been let out of prison. No parents, no siblings, no one telling me what to do or where to be. I spent some nights just walking around the campus.

Living on a Christian campus didn't keep us from drinking. Like all teenagers, Christian or not, we always found a place off-campus where we could party and talk about Jesus, God, and whether we really had to wait until we were married to have sex. I wasn't even sure I was actually a Christian. Though I had been raised Presbyterian, I felt no affiliation with Jesus, Christianity, or the church. I was a free, wandering soul, open to any and all experiences.

It was after two a.m. when I walked into the dorm room I shared with three other guys. The salty smell of dried sweat clung to the clothes piled in the corner. The linoleum floor had a grit of dirt and sand. We didn't have a broom or the desire to use one.

I traded my coat, jeans, and shirt for sweats pulled from the pile on the floor. I opened the door to the room where my suite-mates were sleeping, and the odor that hit me was anything but sweet.

Freshman college boys have a rank odor that can wrinkle your nose and bring tears to your eyes. I slid open the window, pulled the hood of my sweatshirt down over my head, burrowed under the covers, and tried to sleep.

I tossed and turned and tried to ignore the snoring and heavy breathing in our small, cramped room. Mike, one of my roommates, was prone to nightmares. The first night, he screamed as if a knife had been thrust into his gut. We all sat bolt upright, gasping at his midnight rants. As we grew used to sleeping in such tight quarters and to his night terrors, I found that I could just reach across the tight aisle that divided us and jostle him awake and he would calm down, mumble something under his breath, roll over, and go back to sleep. As I lay there that night, my breath fell into the rhythm of my roommates and I slept.

He was suddenly standing in front of me. Jesus—bold and clear. He didn't look like the Jesus in any paintings or movies, but I knew that it was he. I also knew that it wasn't a dream. Jesus was crystal clear and I felt wide awake. But I was not in bed, and instead of roommates, I was surrounded by light—a cosmic light, a creation light. Jesus was in front of me but he wasn't alone.

Behind Jesus stood every pastor I had ever known. There were the two pastors from my childhood church who bored me to tears when I was a child. There were the pastor from the Methodist church that my dad took me to when I was a teenager, the kindly old pastor from my grandmother's church who had baptized me, and the two pastors from another Presbyterian church that we attended when my parents were trying to find a church home. There they were, a stodgy, boring crew, gawking over Jesus's shoulder. My parents, my five siblings, aunts, uncles, and grandparents stood behind the pastors as if they had been summoned to attend a great event.

8

Beyond them, stretching back to the far ends of the cosmic light, was every soul in all of creation. Jesus stood at the point of the crowd like the headpin in a bowling alley. The entire creation fanned out behind him.

I stood across from Jesus and I stood alone.

Jesus slowly raised his arm, pointed at me, and said, "You will be a minister to my people." Jesus let his arm fall to his side. Silence— nothing in all of creation moved. It was as if the world waited for a reply.

He pointed at me again and said, "You will be a minister to my people." His outstretched arm paused and then came to rest by his side. Again, all of creation was silent, watching, bearing witness to what was happening.

Jesus raised his arm a third time, pointed at me, and said, "You will be a minister to my people." The pastors, my family, and all of creation smiled as if in agreement with what Jesus was saying. The silence became a cosmic blessing of sorts. Then Jesus smiled and left.

I startled awake, sat up, and threw off the blankets. The night air from the open window chilled the room. What had just happened? Was I awake? Was I sleeping? What had I seen? Jesus standing in front of me was as vivid as the bodies of my roommates curled under their blankets. The light—where did that light come from? The pastors, my family, all of creation, standing there staring at me— what did their presence in my dream mean?

Jesus pointing at me. At me! I'm eighteen. I'm a *freshman*, for Pete's sake! A minister to his people? What? How? In what way? Was I to be part of that stodgy crew of ministers gathered behind Jesus? Please, dear God, let it not be so! I hated going to church. I wanted to be a lawyer, to argue the law and make big bucks.

My brain raced from Jesus, to the pastors, to my family, to all of creation. I went to the window, leaned out, and breathed in the night air. I had no idea what had happened. I had no idea what it meant. But I knew that Jesus had come, pointed at me, and directed my life.

That was thirty-two years ago. Since then, I've been to seminary and earned a doctorate. For thirty years I've served a church where my passion and energy have been focused on touching the lives of my members in all stages of their faith. I have read deeply into the world's great religions. I have worshiped with Muslims and meditated with Buddhists. I have taught, prayed, and spoken to thousands, all in an effort to understand and fulfill what Jesus meant when he said, "You will be a minister to my people."

In retrospect, I now believe that the Ultimate Being revealed to me that I had been sent. It didn't mean that I was going to be the pope, the next Billy Graham, or some great scholar; it just meant that I had been sent, and it was going to be up to me to figure out the specifics.

My second visitation came in midlife, from the Hindu goddess Lakshmi, the goddess of wealth, prosperity, and abundance. At the time of this visitation I knew little about Hinduism. I had studied the basic concepts of Brahman and atman; I had read the Bhagavad Gita, but outside of Krishna, I was unaware of the Hindu pantheon of gods and how they reflected the magnificent presence of Brahman in the world.

Again, it was late at night. It felt like a dream, but more than a dream. There was a complete awareness that transcended sleep. In this state of awareness I was walking through a forest. From the depths of the woods an owl flew down and alighted on my shoulder. The owl whispered in my ear, "You have been sent for a very important reason." The owl then transformed into a woman seated across from me at a table. The woman wore a hood over her head, but deep brown locks tumbled down around her face. Her eyes sparkled a vivid blue and a bright iridescent red gown shown beneath her brown robe.

Her features were sharp, but warm. She brought out from her gown cards with written instructions and said, "This is what you are to do." I looked at the cards but they were written in Sanskrit. I told the woman that I was unsure what she wanted me to do or say, as I couldn't read the instructions. The woman smiled and said, "Do not worry, everything you need to know is right here." She then reached across the table and with her index finger touched my cosmic third eye in the middle of my forehead. She then smiled and disappeared.

I awoke from the dream/vision with an amazing sense of clarity, yet was completely confused as to what the dream meant. Who was this woman in the dream? I went to my computer and googled, "owls, woman, purpose, dreams." I was overwhelmed by the responses. Owls are a predominant metaphor in so many cultures. As I was reading though, one link struck a chord. It stated, "In the Hindu faith, the goddess Lakshmi is sent by Brahman into the world as his messenger. She enters in the earthly realm on the back of an owl, or in the form of an owl." Beside the definition was a link to the image of Lakshmi. Curious, I clicked the tab. I was startled when a picture of the woman in my dream, Lakshmi, opened!

Since then I have done a tremendous amount of reading about Lakshmi. As a Christian, I still have only a thumbnail understanding of the wonder of this amazing goddess. The Hindu faith understands her as the goddess of wealth and prosperity. She is worshiped in a wonderful celebration called Deepavali, a festival of lights held in mid-October or mid-November. Lakshmi's avatar depicts her sitting in a lotus position, her hands open with gold coins spilling from them. She is revered not so much for the material wealth that she presents as for the great abundance and generosity of Brahman to the world.

I was deeply honored and challenged to have had this visitation. According to her avatar, Brahman sent her to deliver a message to me. Did it mean that I was to become a Hindu priest? Was I to be the next great incarnation of Krishna? Hardly . . . I struggle with just understanding Christianity, let alone following Jesus. But it confirmed in my being for a second time that I had been sent. The Cosmic Being, whether called Allah, Brahman, God, or Tao, had sent me into the world to do something significant.

Jesus's purpose for my life has taken many shapes and forms over the years. I have meditated and worked to understand and live out what Lakshmi charged me to do. Along this journey I have stumbled, failed, and had some success. But most importantly . . .

I have learned.

I have learned what it means to be sent and how to empower people to discover how and why the Creator sent them. It is my desire that this book be like Jesus pointing at your soul, calling you by name, telling you that you are here for a reason. I pray that this book may be like Lakshmi pointing to your forehead, telling you that Brahman has sent you for a great destiny. May you choose to engage this exciting adventure and discover why you have been sent!

As you have sent me into the world,
so I have sent them into the world.

—John 17:18

Chapter One

The Goo That Is You

The Creator of the universe sent you. This may be a hard notion to wrap your head around; however, when you allow this notion to settle into your bones it changes everything about you. It means that, instead of being a mere human living an average existence, you have a holy destiny—there is something you are to do.

Too often people feel that they have lived a successful day if they have managed to commute through traffic to work, shuffle along until noon, struggle to make it until 5 p.m., go home, eat dinner, watch a few hours of television, and go to bed, only to start the whole process over again the next day. These days become weeks, months, and then years. People spend their whole lives walking paths that soon become ruts, which eventually lead to graves. All the while they are oblivious to the notion that they have been sent to the world to accomplish something marvelous.

Have you ever felt agitated because you know in your heart that there has to be more to life than what you're currently doing? But you have this job; you have a mortgage, insurance, and bills to pay. Maybe you have a family that depends upon you and your income; so you feel that you're stuck. But you know that you are not using your true gifts and abilities. This feeling is the Divine's way of saying, "Yes, there is more I want you to do!" Your desire for *more* indicates that there is a higher potential, a greater dream you need to fulfill.

The Christian New Testament tells many stories of people the Creator sent into the world. Jesus was sent into the world. The

CHAPTER ONE

Gospel of John makes this abundantly clear. Jesus was not just living a normal day-to-day existence; there was a purpose, a destiny that Jesus was to fulfill. Jesus was sent to be the Messiah and usher in the Kingdom of God.

Jesus knew this, and that knowledge shaped his understanding of his reason for existing. He knew that he had been sent, and he repeatedly said this to those around him. Before he raised Lazarus from the dead, in front of the crowds that had gathered, Jesus looked to the heavens and spoke to God: "I knew that you always hear me, but I have said this for the sake of the crowd standing here, so that they may believe that *you sent me*."[1] When Jesus was teaching that he was the bread of life, he said, "The Father *who sent me* is in charge."[2] Jesus knew that his life was not ordinary. He was on a divine mission and this mission shaped everything about him. It shaped his thoughts, how he spent his time, and how he worked with others.

The Creator also sent the apostle Paul. Paul knew that the great Cosmic Entity had chosen him for a special mission and had a unique intention for his life. When Paul's life was turned around on the road to Damascus, Paul knew that he was to take the Gospel of Jesus to the Gentile world. Everything about Paul's life was shaped by his divine purpose.

Paul constantly informed anyone listening that God had sent him, "Paul an apostle—*sent* neither by human commission nor from human authorities, but through Jesus Christ and God the Father."[3] This purpose filled him with passion; since he knew that he had been sent, it empowered him to endure ridicule, torture, and imprisonment. Much as happened with Jesus, Paul's purpose shaped his thinking, it shaped how he spent his time, and it shaped the people he spent time with.

The Jewish scriptures also tell many stories of the Creator acting in the world. HaShem sent the prophet Jeremiah into the world, saying to him, "Before I formed you in the womb I knew you, and before you were born I consecrated you; I appointed you a prophet to the nations."[4] There was a divine intention for Jeremiah's life. He was to be HaShem's spokesperson.

Throughout the Jewish and Christian scriptures, the Creator chose people to send on holy missions. Hindus believe that Brahman sent Krishna. In the Bhagavad Gita, Krishna tells Arjuna that in times of crises he is sent by Brahman into the world. Islam teaches that Allah sent Mohammed to be the one to reveal the final truth. The Baha'i faith teaches that God sends many different prophets and teachers at different times in human history. My point here is not to argue the plurality of religions, but to point out a common element of many of the great faiths: the Creator *sends* people into the world.

The question is, are these heroes of the world's religions unique? Are they set aside as a few holy examples that were sent into the world? There are some who argue for this point. Many people believe that Moses, Jesus, Paul, Mohammed, and Krishna are unique examples. I disagree. Making these people exceptions, asserting that they are the only ones who have been sent, limits not only the message of these sacred scriptures, but also the way in which the Ultimate Being works in the world.

This is the pivotal point—once you accept the concept that these spiritual giants represent the pattern for the workings of the Creator, it's like a marvelous key slipping into a lock, opening up a whole new meaning of existence. Suddenly, the words of Jesus take on a deep significance. Instead of Jesus speaking of the disciples, Jesus is speaking of you when he says, "As you have sent me into the world, so have I sent them into the world."[5] When you read this verse, do you feel the hand of Jesus pointing at you? You are the "them" that Jesus is talking about, you and every other person in the world. As the Creator sent Jesus, Paul, Krishna, and Mohammad on a holy mission, you are anointed in the same way. You need to hear the words of Jesus ring in your heart. The Creator *sends* you. It's the pattern, the dream, and the way the Cosmic Being works.

Preknowing

Once you accept this divine pattern, amazing concepts begin to form. You begin to realize that the Creator has not merely chosen you, but, before you were even conceived, placed a divine intention within you.

The Christian New Testament speaks of God preknowing you. In the book of Romans, Paul writes that God "foreknew" us.[6] In Ephesians the author writes that "before the foundation of the world" you were chosen to be holy and blameless.[7] Before you were born, before you were conceived, there was some divine cooking going on. In the Jewish scriptures, the psalmist says, "Your eyes have seen my unformed substance."[8]

Do this. Take out your smart phone, hold it at arm's distance and take a picture of yourself. Wherever you are in life—thirties, midfifties, late seventies, it doesn't matter; just look at yourself and contemplate the notion that you are here for a reason. Your life has amazing potential yet to be realized.

Now let's take a journey back in your life. Go back in your mind's eye to when you were eighteen. You just graduated from high school. Think about your life then. You had the world by the tail, and you were glad to finally be out of high school. You had amazing things you wanted to do. People told you that you had so much potential and you knew you could be anything that you wanted to be.

But let's not stop there; go back even further. Go back to the day you were born. Your parents looked at you with great hopes and dreams for your life. Again, you had potential; it was unrealized, waiting within you.

Take another step back. Imagine yourself as an embryo in your mother's womb. What potential did you hold then? I believe you were raw and developing energy. Your arms and legs were being fashioned and knit together, and so were your gifts, skills, and abilities. Take another step back; go back to when you were a sperm on the edge of penetrating an egg. Did "you" even exist? Yes. While your physical body had not been formed, this sperm and egg were part of the dream the Creator had for you.

Let's take one more step back in your creation process. Is there another step back? According to the psalmist, there is. Before your physical presence, there was the divine thought of you, a light and a luminescence. The Creator held your "unformed substance," the goo that was to become you. You were consecrated for something. Gifts were planted deep within you, as were holy destinies and purposes. These purposes were embedded into your beginning; then you were *sent* into the creation. As your body was knit together in your mother's womb, these gifts and skills became part of your DNA. Your raw potential began to take shape with each day of your embryonic development. The day of your birth was a great celebration, not just because you entered the world, but because the divine dreams for your life began.

Now, fast-forward to where you are right now, holding your picture on your smart phone. Ponder the process we have just imagined. The Creator made you. Like a newly composed song or a sculpture carved in clay, your body was gloriously made. But more than just building your bones, muscles, and organs, the Cosmic Being held you like a luminescent ball and planted your destiny within you. There is a purpose behind your creation, a holy mission for your existence. Your life is not just an egg and a sperm coming together, but an act of God.

This is exactly what HaShem was saying to Jeremiah:

> Before I formed you in the womb
> I knew you,
> And before you were born
> I consecrated you;
> I appointed you a prophet to the nations.[9]

Jeremiah's destiny is clearly laid before him. It wasn't just his body that was made; it was his identity and destiny as well. Is Jeremiah's creation the exception or the pattern? I believe it is the pattern. The Creator held the core essence of Jeremiah, Jesus, and Paul, and it held your core essence as well. Jesus was consecrated to be the Messiah to the world. Paul was consecrated to be the evangelist to the Gentiles, and Jeremiah was consecrated to be a prophet to the nations. What about you?

The Guiding Principle

The stellar insight is that many of the major world religions mirror this same concept. They express a central truth behind religion and spirituality; the guiding principle for the Cosmic Being is to send people into the world to fulfill particular destinies.

Hinduism

Within Hinduism the Ultimate Being is called Brahman, the grand creator, the cosmic light and pure love that has existed from the beginning of creation. Brahman is very active in the creation and permeates the world, atman, in infinite ways. The soul, or *jivatman*, of each human being is uniquely connected to Brahman. Brahman and atman are different, yet one; separate yet connected. From the beginning of a person's incarnation, Brahman has preknown the individual for unique purposes. The jivatman is imbedded with a holy purpose, a unique set of destinies, and specific gifts to fulfill this destiny. This holy purpose is the person's dharma.

Dharma is the life force that drives an individual forward in life, filling a person with the sense that they are supposed to do something with this lifetime. Dharma compels a person to search, to become educated, and to choose to fulfill that for which Brahman created them. A person who is not aligned with his or her dharma is not satisfied with life. The major theme that runs throughout the Bhagavad Gita is that if you are living your dharma, you have found bliss. However, if you have chosen to live counter to your dharma you are unsatisfied and unfulfilled.[10]

Brahman intentionally sends people into the world. A human is not just created and plopped into existence with the expectation that he or she will grow and flounder into adulthood and perchance discover a sense of meaning. No; before the human is conceived, it is Brahman's intention that this life will serve a unique purpose.

Taoism

The ancient Chinese religion Taoism refers to the Ultimate Being as the Tao. Instead of dharma, Taoists refer to the power of the Tao embedded in a person as the person's *te*. When a person lives in the midst of te, that person's actions are smooth and effortless. This state of being is called *wu-wei*, literally, "not doing."

The Tao is that which is beyond words. It is so grand that ultimately it cannot be explained or described. There is no name that captures the true essence of the Tao. It is the Tao that created the universe, this planet, and your life. While massive, the Tao is also present and known. It flows through the world as a cosmic force. It thrives in the wilderness as well as in city streets. It is as smooth as a babbling brook and as grand as a tsunami. Each human being is connected to the great Tao and is filled with it. A person finds satisfaction and happiness in life by allowing the Tao to move through him or her. When one discovers what one is naturally supposed to do, one has unleashed te.

Te is the power of the Tao embodied. Before a human is conceived, the Tao is embedded as something akin to a genetic code within the soul. This code holds the gifts and skills a person needs to thrive and creates the uniqueness of each individual. From the moment of birth the Tao grows and matures. The Tao of the individual merges with the Tao of others and that of the world. The great challenge is to align your life with the way in which the Tao is moving. The more you strive to do something you were not created for, the more dissatisfied you become. However, if you relax and do what is natural for you, what the Tao has sent you for, you find not only satisfaction, but te. Your life is full of power and potential. Te guides your life like the North Star. It empowers you to choose rightly in complex situations. If you are living your te, you do not force your life; it unfolds according to the purpose of the great Tao. When you are expressing te you often step into a flow, a groove, where your actions seem effortless. It is action, nonaction; it is wu-wei.

Judaism

The roots of Judaism go back to the ancient Hebrew people of the first and second millennia BCE. For Jewish people, the name of the deity is sacred and cannot be uttered. It is often referred to simply as HaShem, which means "the Name." HaShem is the power of the Tao embodied. As Brahman created the world in its vastness, so did HaShem. As stories abound about Brahman's creative abilities, so do they about HaShem. While Hindus disagree whether there is one God or hundreds of thousands of gods, the Jewish people are very clear: there is one God, HaShem.

HaShem chose the ancient Hebrews to be his sacred people. The Nation of Judah was to be the living example of HaShem's presence on earth. The first human was created when HaShem blew his breath, the Ruach, the sacred wind, into Adam. Adam was created in the image of HaShem, as were all subsequent human beings. The psalmists, the Hebrew poets, say that HaShem holds the luminescence of an individual's soul. The body is carefully knit together. Each bone and sinew marveled over. Each person is given gifts, skills, and abilities. The Hebrews, individually and collectively, were chosen and sent by HaShem into the world. While HaShem raised up kings and prophets to guide the nation, each Hebrew is a sacred part of HaShem's family. Each has a unique place in the community of faith. The purpose of an individual life is to fulfill this unique role. Everyone from the lowliest orphan to the eldest widow is needed to express the justice, mercy, and love of HaShem.

Christianity

Christianity grew out of Judaism. The deity moves from a name that is never uttered, to one that is personal and intimate, God the Father. But more than father, Jesus referred to God the Father in intimate ways, such as "Abba," which literally translated means "Dad" or "Daddy." Christianity teaches that Jesus is the Son of God and that the Creator sent Jesus into the world to serve as the Jewish Messiah. This is where Jews and Christians part ways.

Christians believe that the life of Jesus was larger than Judaism, as his resurrection saved the entire world. The mission of Jesus is continued through those that follow him. Jesus taught that as God sent him into the world, so Jesus sends his disciples into the world to spread the good news of God's love and grace. The same divine spirit that was in Jesus is also in every one of his followers. There is a divine unity that binds all of the disciples, Jesus, and God together. The individual Christian must use free will to accept the gift of God's grace and to further Jesus's mission.

All humans have spiritual gifts. Their purpose is to discern their gifts and to use their free will to choose for God's purpose in the creation. God has a plan for each human life. When the plan is followed, it brings hope to the person's life and establishes the Kingdom of God on earth. As humans realize that God sent them to fulfill a unique destiny, they collaborate with God, bringing about the next phase of the creation.

Baha'i

A relatively new religion, second only to Christianity in its global scope, is the Baha'i faith. The Baha'i religion holds that there is one divine presence, God, from which all of the world religions have emanated. Throughout the centuries God has sent unique manifestations to lead and guide the world. Lao Tzu, Krishna, Abraham, Jesus, and Mohammed are reflections of such manifestations. The most recent manifestation is the Baha'u'llah.

The history of the Baha'i faith reaches beyond the Baha'u'llah to the Babi movement in Iran. In 1844 a young man named Siyyid Mírzá `Alí-Muhammad claimed to be the fulfillment and redeemer of the Islamic faith. He called himself the B`ab, literally meaning "the Gate." The B`ab acquired many followers across the Persian Empire, who were persecuted for their beliefs. He was eventually executed by firing squad in 1850. Before his death, the B`ab taught that God was going to send an ultimate manifestation to carry on this new movement. The

24

B`ab referred to him as "the One whom God shall make manifest." This promised one would establish the kingdom of God on earth. After the B`ab's death, one of his passionate followers, Mírzá Husayn-`Alí Núrí, was recognized as this promised one and took on the name Baha'u'llah, which literally means "the Glory of God."[11]

The Baha'u'llah was a progressive individual with great insight. Many contemporary theologies mirror his teachings. He taught that the human race was one entity and all the world should be unified. All differences between classes and religions should be eliminated. He taught that each individual is also a manifestation of God created in God's sacred image. As each individual is created, unique gifts and abilities are planted at the core level of the person's being. The Baha'u'llah refers to the gifts within each person as a gold mine of possibilities. Life's purpose is for each person to develop these gifts. Fulfilling one's purpose brings to fruition the many attributes of God. Each individual life is crucial; together they all empower the world to advance toward fulfillment.

New Age

The contemporary New Age religions express this same concept in a variety of ways. New Age beliefs developed as people became confused and frustrated with the dogmatism of the world's religions, whose adherents have battled with one another, each claiming to have the divine truth. New Age spirituality goes beyond religious structures. New Age believers often describe themselves as "spiritual but not religious." Yet, within the broad scope of New Age beliefs there are also references to being sent by a Divine Presence.

According to New Age teachings, if you can still the noise in your life, if your are able to hush the frantic pace of moving to and fro, if you can just "be" in the moment, you will feel the movement of the universe within you. This sacred presence awakens you to your divine essence. It dawns upon you that, more than being just a simple human, you are uniquely connected to the universe. The beat of your heart is the rhythm of the universe that created the cosmos from the beginning. Any disconnection you feel from the universe stems from your own misunderstanding. When your body quiets, your soul leads you back to your divine beginning. You can see that, just as a holy purpose is guiding the universe forward toward enlightenment, so is your life guiding you. You understand that your existence is not an accident, but is filled with purpose and action. The universe has sent you here for a reason. The great desire and goal of a human life is to discover why the universe has sent you and to choose to embody it in your life.

The great mistake people make is when they live small lives. The universe sent them for a great reason and they need to live boldly. You find satisfaction when you realize that, more than having a soul, you *are* a soul. Your life is sacred, a miracle, as you participate in the great unfolding of the cosmic purpose.

Buddhism

Buddhism does not recognize a relational divine being like the God of the Abrahamic religions or Brahman within Hinduism. However, Buddhism does hold a key element that directly influences our divine destiny—the power of choice. Buddhism teaches that there is a cosmic purpose for each life. That purpose is to choose to live with compassion, responding to the suffering of the world, teaching the dharma as one encounters each moment of existence. The Dalai Lama, the spiritual leader of Tibetan Buddhists, said that the central role of the Buddhist is to think critically and act accordingly. Through our right choices we develop positive karma, which propels us toward our next incarnation, ultimately leading to enlightenment.

The notion of appropriate choices is critical in discerning why we have been sent. Within each moment there are a myriad of decisions that must be made. The Buddhist Eightfold path teaches that there is a "right" way to think, act, work, speak, et cetera, that allows the individual to respond appropriately within the context of life. The Buddhist believes that we must make choices that are "right" for each moment. It is this teaching of right choices that is central to us as we bring the divine dream to fruition.

Summary of the Guiding Principle

The world religions differ profoundly from one another. Each has a unique vision of life's ultimate purpose. Within each religion there is a vast spectrum of beliefs; many would disagree with my simplistic descriptions. Yet, among these great faiths I discern a pattern. There is a Divine Being that for some is relational. For others it is a vast Cosmic Purpose. This Holy Other has an intention and a purpose for the creation. Its presence is imbedded and moves throughout all of the cosmos. Humans are a critical part of this unfolding drama. As one lives, develops, and chooses to act, one not only discovers one's reason for being but also collaborates with the Creator to accomplish a great and glorious purpose.

The question becomes, how are you a part of this unfolding picture? Are you collaborating with the movement of the Creator or are you wasting your precious life on something that twists and turns but ultimately leads to a dead end, a cul-de-sac of the soul? All of these world religions, their founders and adherents, while disagreeing on many aspects of belief, would all agree on one central insight—you must wake up and embody the sacred aspect of your life. The world needs what you were sent here to offer.

Where Are You Pouring Your Life?

You are here for a reason! It is clear that the Creator shaped you, formed you, and sent you. So what are you doing about it? Like a jug pouring out water, are you pouring yourself out in such a way that your divine destiny is realized?

I'm amazed at how people pour themselves out for things that ultimately lead them nowhere. They invest thousands of dollars and a great deal of energy and emotions in cul-de-sacs of the soul. For instance, when I hear people talking incessantly about television shows they watch each evening, I think to myself, "Is television a reflection of their destiny?" When I see people pour their souls into being sports fans for particular teams with a fervor that equals that of the most ardent religious zealot, I ask myself . . .

is this really why the Creator sent them?

Do the time, passion, and energy people pour into these things bring them closer to a cosmic awareness? Do they further the creation? Is it this person's destiny to be a raging fan of the Minnesota Vikings, a faithful follower of Meryl Streep, or a dedicated listener to U2? Did the Creator really hold the seed of this human soul and say, "Ahh, I'm sending this person into the world to be the number one fan of American Idol!"

No! You were not sent to fritter away your time. Here's the deal: If you can say with certainty that television, surfing the net, or cheering for your team is fulfilling your divine destiny, then that's your prerogative. But if you picked up this book because you have a strong sense that there is something else for your life, then I say that every moment, every dollar, every ounce of emotion you pour into something else is a distraction from your purpose.

Of course, we need to relax and enjoy recreation. I become concerned, and I believe that the Creator becomes concerned, when that recreation becomes the reason for existence—when the sports team provides meaning and bread for the journey of life; when following a movie star provides a sense of identity; and when someone else's music becomes the only rhythm of your soul.

I believe the world would change if people woke up to why they were sent, if they dedicated their lives to discerning their destiny, and if they used their gifts. Poverty would be addressed, cures would be found, and oppressors would be confronted. It may sound a little lofty, but this is why the Creator sends people into the world . . .

to address these challenges.

Many believe that people like Mother Theresa, Gandhi, and Martin Luther King Jr., are unique individuals—that each was sent into the world to fulfill a special purpose—and I agree. However, they are really no different from you and me. They were unique because they spent the time to discern their destiny and had the courage to embody it in their lives.

You may not be here to work with the poor in Calcutta, for the freedom of India, or for civil rights in the United States. Your destiny may be as a mother, a father, a plumber, or a police officer. Your purpose may evolve over the span of your life. It's not one concrete plan that the Creator has for your life, but *plans* that spin and change. I'll talk more about this in later chapters. The point is that you have been sent into the world to make a profound impact on human existence.

So, for what purpose are you pouring yourself out? If you deeply desire to unleash your divine potential, you may need to change. You may need to turn off the television, get off Facebook, and put down the murder mystery. Get busy understanding the purpose for which the Cosmic Being preknew you.

The function of almost all religions is to enable individuals to find union with the Creator. Some teach this connection through prayer and meditation, others through community worship; all of these practices allow people to step into the holy presence. Additionally, if you spend time and take risks to embody the reason you were sent, the connection you'll feel will be profound. You will know that your life and work are an extension of the divine hand in the world.

You will be able to say, as Jesus said, "We are energetically at work for the One who sent me here."[12] When you realize that your life is a holy mission, then Paul's words are yours: "[I am] an apostle—*sent* neither by human commission nor from human authorities, but through Jesus Christ and God the Father."[13] Your challenge is to discover your destiny and pour out your life, bringing it to fulfillment.

Questions to Help You Discover and Explore Your Divine Purpose

1. What is your name for the Creator? How do you react when someone refers to it by another name? Does it offend you or broaden your understanding?

2. What faith tradition do your adhere to? Do you know anyone from another faith background? Have you worshiped with

someone of a religious tradition other than your own? What was that experience like?

3. For what purpose are you pouring out your life? Do you find meaning in the way you spend your time, or do you feel as if there is something more that you are supposed to be doing with your life?

4. Do you believe that God sends people into the world? Do you believe that God sent Jesus, the apostle Paul, Moses, Abraham, the Buddha, Mohammed, and Krishna? If you believe that God did not send these people, how did they rise to their significance? If you do believe that God sent them, when did God plant within them their life purpose?

5. If God sent these spiritual giants, are they the exception to the way God works in the world, or are they the example, the pattern for the way God works in the world? What do you believe about preknowing? Do you believe that God preknows us? If not, how do you account for our innate gifts and proclivities? If yes, what do you believe that God preknew you for? How do you know this?

6. What is it, or who is it in your life, that is holding you back from fulfilling your destiny? If it's a person, then name him or her. How did this person get into your life? Is it a family member or did you choose this person to be a part of your life? How are you going to unravel yourself from this relationship?

   If it is a situation that is keeping you from fulfilling your destiny, then name it as well. How did you get into this situation? What is keeping you stuck here? What is it going to take to free you from its grip?

Now to him who by the power at work within us is able to accomplish abundantly far more than all we can ask or imagine . . .

—Ephesians 3:20

Chapter Two

The Dream Stream

Maybe you're reading this book from a hospital bed. Chemotherapy drips from an IV bag like acid from an old car battery and you're thinking, "The Creator has sent me for this? Right. I'm sitting here fighting cancer. My hair has fallen out and my bones feel as brittle as stale pretzels. If I have been sent, then cancer has stomped on my purpose like a boot to the toes."

It could be that you found this book while you were standing in line for food stamps. Or you saw it in the clinic waiting room. You flipped through it and thought, "I'm unemployed, I'm one rent check away from being homeless, I have two kids to feed, and someone is telling me that the Ultimate Being has sent me? How naïve!"

Life dishes out tragedies, challenges, and chaos, and we have no option but to eat what has been set before us. I have no idea about the suffering you are enduring, but I do know that you were not sent into the world to suffer.

The Creator does not preknow people for trauma and pain. Instead these experiences are the accidents that come crashing into our lives. Sometimes they are the result of our poor choices. Sometimes they are a part of the natural biology of living organisms in a dynamic world. It is not the will of the Creator for you to suffer from cancer or face unemployment.

God's will . . . we toss off the phrase "God's will be done" as if we are fated to live in the particular circumstances in which we find ourselves. We stand with our tragedies and challenges as if we were standing before a divine judge who had just handed down a holy decree, "This is my will, let it be done to your life." We take the decree and are shackled to whatever the holy judge has given us. For some it's prison or poverty, for others, wealth and riches. For a sacred being who has sent us to fulfill a divine destiny, this seems capricious.

I believe the exact opposite. Instead of the divine will being a whimsical, capricious desire under which we suffer or to which we acquiesce, it is a presence that works, creates, and overcomes the challenges we face. The will of the Creator is not a decree to which we bow, but a force that lives through us. As the author of Ephesians from the Christian New Testament states, God's power is "at work within us."[1] In each tragedy that we face, this divine agency is working to change our oppressive circumstances.

Leslie Weatherhead, in his marvelous book *The Will of God*, describes this will as having three distinct phases: an intentional will, a circumstantial will, and an ultimate will.[2] Weatherhead uses the metaphor of a stream flowing down a mountain to describe these three phases.

The Flow of God's Will

To understand the *intentional will*, picture a beautiful stream starting at the top of a mountain. The original intention for the stream is that it have a smooth, bright journey down the mountain. The stream is crystal clear, its banks are lined with ferns; it is filled with trout that swim and splash. The Creator intends that deer, raccoons, and nuthatches come to the stream, drink from it, and find sustenance. The stream flows to its ultimate conclusion—joining other streams in a mighty river at the valley floor. This is the divine intentional will.

The second phase, the *circumstantial will*, is when circumstances dam the flow of the stream. These circumstances are cascading rocks, branches, and logs, or pollution dumped in by factories. Eventually the stream becomes so muddy and filled with debris that the flow stops altogether. The stream and those trying to enjoy it could say, "The divine original intention is lost. Its sacred destiny is destroyed and the Holy One has abandoned the stream."

What the stream and those sitting on its banks fail to realize is that a living, dynamic force is inherent in the stream, pushing against the circumstances that have dammed its flow. This force does not stop until the purpose of the stream has been realized.

The Ultimate Being sees no stream as dead. It created the stream, and its presence now lives amidst the rocks, logs, and pollution. Even while the stream is completely dammed and appears dead, the cosmic power resides within it.

This force in the stream is dynamic. It uses each circumstance, each obstacle, to further its intention. The force pushes against the obstacles. Its presence purifies the pollution that has poured into the stream. When the sacred love of justice is frustrated, the force in the stream is unsettled and angry that the destiny of the stream is blocked.

The Creator amps up the force and the stream pushes all the harder; it desires to participate in the joy of its original intent. The sacred desire for justice attracts other divine forces to increase the flow of the stream, and humans to work to unclog the dam. The Creator digs new channels for the stream. Instead of going straight down the mountain, the stream may now veer to the right or to the left.

The stream may have to wait, sometimes for a very long time, to overcome all the obstacles. The Creator does not rest or retreat until it has achieved the purpose for which the stream was *sent* down the mountainside.

The *ultimate will* of the Creator is fulfilled when the stream overcomes all obstacles. A channel is formed and the stream resumes its flow. Fish thrive, animals come to drink, and ferns, moss, and shrubs line the stream's banks. The stream makes wonderful music as it achieves its ultimate goal—to join all other streams and form a mighty river. This stream is your life, your destiny, and the reason you were sent.

The Intentional Will

When you were created, when the Ultimate Being preknew you and set you on the course of your life, this intentional will was planted in your soul. You were intended to find joy and love. You were to bask in an abundance of blessings, to experience justice, fairness, and wholeness, so that the reason you were sent would ultimately be fulfilled. Then you were flung into the creation and you were born . . . and this is where your joys and trouble began.

The Circumstantial Will

The hands that welcome some infants are wonderful and nurturing. Other infants, even before their first breath, encounter poverty, pollution, and injustice. Some infants experience joy, love, and abundance, and others fight for their very existence. The divine original intention flourishes for some, and for others the circumstances of life crash into them before they are even moments old.

As a child grows, its life dips and diverges like a rollercoaster. Ideally, the original intention for a child is nurtured and blessed by parents who surround it with a room full of books and toys, a warm bed to be tucked into, and a table full of macaroni and wieners. For others, the circumstances bash against them throughout their lives.

When the child becomes an adolescent, the original intention is nurtured by high schools that create thriving communities of learning. Its divine purpose is teased out by those who teach because teaching is the purpose for which they were sent into the world. These people instinctively know how to guide and prod students to enjoy their natural gifts.

For some, however, adolescence is nothing but one painful, pimple-faced rejection after another. They sit in the back of the classroom and try to hide their broken souls. They are spat on in the bus, they are raped, and they are abused. They hide their depression behind a boozy haze from Old Turkey snuck from the family's liquor cabinet.

After high school the intentional will blossoms into a full-grown passion, leading young adults into college or careers. Professors, who are on the planet to inspire people, expand their students' brains with knowledge and cognitive skills, classrooms and labs. They can point young adults on paths that empower them to fully realize their sacred potential. Other young adults discover skills that allow them to bypass college and dive into sales, mechanics, or parenting, all of which are second nature to them, innate from the Creator.

For many, the stage of young adulthood is when the circumstances of life whack into them. Many young adults are ill-prepared to join the workaday world. They stagger under the weight of jobs, insurance, rent, groceries, and bosses who abuse their youthful naïveté. A best friend is killed in a violent car crash. For the first time, many young adults struggle for meaning when circumstances dam their stream to a standstill.

Life flourishes and flounders. It rises like a hawk and lands like a buzzard. If you live long enough, eventually something goes wrong. You flip a switch and a small spark in an outlet smolders. In the middle of the night the smoke alarm blares, you jerk awake to the smell of smoke. You grope your way out of the house with your kids in tow and stand helpless as your home, with all your irreplaceable treasures, goes up in flames. The circumstances of life can be flat-out devastating.

. . . Yet the Cosmic Being pushes.

The One who originally held you, holds you still. The Creator is with a child left in a garbage bin, a teenager's painful and lonely tears, the despair of a young adult wallowing in debt, and finally, the utter defeat that comes from the catastrophes of life. Like the force in the stream that pushes against the rocks and logs until a new course is dug, so the divine will pushes your life forward.

Barry's life was devastated by financial ruin. When Wall Street collapsed in the economic downturn, Barry lost it all. His 401K became a 201K overnight, and Barry's employer could no longer afford to employ him. He had been a top college graduate with two masters degrees, earning close to six figures, and he was suddenly unemployed. He burned through his savings in six months while he looked for a job. Creditors demanding payment hounded him. His house was foreclosed on and his belongings put out on the street. He was lost and homeless.

That was until Barry talked with Jane, a local realtor, who directed Barry to a lead on a rental. The owner, understanding

Barry's situation, waived the first and last deposits, and Barry had a home for his family.

One day, Barry walked down to the corner coffee shop and was sitting in the sun sipping a latte. He thought that since he was unemployed, and if he had to start over, he would work where his passion was—as a chef. While Barry was sitting there, a man came and sat across from him and they began talking. The man's name was Dan; he was a chef at a local restaurant. He told Barry that they needed additional help in the kitchen. Barry applied and within the week was humming behind the stove at Dan's thriving bistro. Was Barry making a ton of money? No. Was Barry satisfied beyond belief? Yes. As amazing as this story may sound, it's true.

Now, was each of these positive turns of events in Barry's life a coincidence? I say not. I say that these "coincidences" are reflections of the divine will working in the circumstances of life. It never rests, never gives up; it keeps on working until the dam has been broken and the stream begins to flow again.

The Ultimate Will

The ultimate will is like cresting a hill at the moment the sunset splashes color across the sky. It is like the "ahh" that you breathe as you settle into a warm bath or enjoy a glass of a fine Merlot. All of these moments bring a sense of satisfaction reflecting the joy of the ultimate will being realized.

Resurrection, nirvana, enlightenment, oneness, is the ultimate will fully realized. Our joy is complete as we move from death to the next phase of existence. Death is not a tragedy for the Creator, only a transition.

Your circumstances may be Alzheimer's slowly eroding your ability to think and act until you have been reduced to the mental and emotional level of a three-year-old. Your circumstances may blast you through the windshield of a car, erasing your life in the shards of a car wreck. The ways we die are endless. Each of these tragic circumstances is devastating. Our lives are snuffed out. It feels as though the divine will has been thwarted. We are done. The Cosmic Being is done. The divine plan and purpose for our lives have been destroyed.

. . . The opposite is true.

Our death is our ultimate victory. At the moment we die, we step into the glory of the Creator. Depending upon your faith tradition, the tragic circumstances of death bring you to the glorious next phase of existence. In the Christian New Testament the apostle Paul quoted the saying, "'Death has been swallowed up in victory.' 'Where, O death, is thy victory? Where, O death, is thy sting?'"[3] The divine ultimate will is complete when union with the Cosmic Being is achieved. Death, the final circumstance of life, fully realizes our purpose. The Divine One who held our essence, who preknew us for a great destiny, and who sent us into the world, stands at the edge of eternity at the moment of our death with open arms, waiting to hear of our marvelous adventure.

Your circumstances don't change the reason you were sent. These circumstances are like the logs, sticks, and mud that dam the stream. The reason the Creator sent you is not thwarted; its power is pushing right now to bring you to a new day.

Imagine this great force moving on your behalf. When I think of the divine power I like to imagine the Hindu deity Ganesh, who is depicted as an elephant. Ganesh is the remover of obstacles. Before starting any new project, Hindus bow before Ganesh. Before the foundation for a home is laid, they dedicate the building to Ganesh.

When they face a major challenge or problem in life, they turn to Ganesh. Hindus worship Ganesh because they recognize that the elephant represents a massive force that removes the obstacles and challenges they face. It's important to note that Hindus are not worshiping an elephant; they are recognizing the presence of God, Brahman, present within the world as a power that is working on their behalf.

Imagine the force of God working in your life like a majestic elephant. The giant beast leans his head into your problems; his trunk lifts the tree limbs and rocks that block your way. The elephant is persistent in his work and does not stop until your way has been cleared.

Taoism also recognizes the power of God moving through the universe to remove obstacles. The great force of the universe, the Tao, cannot be stopped, moved, or thwarted. Like water that shapes and molds rock, like wind that blows storm fronts, like the mighty forces that lift mountain ranges, so this force moves in our lives.

Taoism teaches that a person must learn how to allow the Tao to move and how to align their actions with the work of the Tao. People must remove their anxieties, let go of their desires, and fill themselves with the presence and movement of the Tao.

As you face the circumstances of your life, imagine the great force of the Tao moving on your behalf. Like a mighty stream, a gale-force wind, the pressure that moves continents, this presence is moving to overcome the obstacles you face.

Imagine this power as it stands against unemployment. Do you think it is intimidated by the loss of a job? No; like the huge head of an elephant, it simply leans itself into this challenge and pushes until the challenge is removed. Has some accident ripped the rug of your life from under you? Do you think that the great presence of the universe is limited in this case? No; like the pressure that is within a river shaping deep canyons, so this presence lifts you to a new place in life.

Ganesh, the great Tao, the Holy Spirit, are wonderful images that represent the way in which the Creator moves through your life. It cannot be stopped, thwarted, maligned, or limited. It simply moves forward. The challenge in the midst of your circumstances is to ask, "How can I use these circumstances to further my divine purpose? How can I open myself to seeing the Creator working in the midst of my challenges?" The story of Joseph from the Jewish scriptures is a beautiful case in point.

Joseph's jealous brothers sold him into slavery. He was taken down to Egypt and bought by Potiphar, an officer of Pharaoh. At this point we might say that HaShem's purpose in sending Joseph into the world was thwarted. Joseph was in some of the worst circumstances imaginable. But he was not alone. The author of Genesis says, "The Lord was with Joseph."[4] In the midst of these tragic circumstances, HaShem was present and working to shape Joseph's life.

Instead of being oppressed by these circumstances Joseph chose to thrive. He worked hard in Potiphar's house and was made overseer. Joseph succeeded in his position, but then another tragedy came his way. Potiphar's wife fell in love with Joseph and wanted to have an affair with him. Joseph repeatedly refused her advances. Potiphar's wife, out of spite, told Potiphar that it was Joseph who had made advances toward her. Potiphar became enraged and threw Joseph into a deep dungeon.

The circumstances of Joseph's life became danker and darker. The author says again, "But the Lord was with Joseph and showed him steadfast love."[5] Joseph refused to give up on himself or HaShem. Joseph continued to act on HaShem's behalf. Joseph interpreted dreams of others who were sent to prison. He languished in his cell for two years, yet HaShem was with him.

In a unique turn of events Pharaoh had a disturbing dream. He was told that Joseph had the ability to interpret dreams, so Joseph was brought from prison to stand before him. Joseph interpreted Pharaoh's dream so successfully that Pharaoh appointed Joseph as the overseer of all of Egypt.

Eventually a famine that Joseph had predicted came to pass, and people from all the surrounding countryside, including Joseph's brothers who had sold him into slavery, came to Egypt for food. When Joseph and his brothers recognized each other, there was a tearful reunion as the brothers confessed and apologized for their wrongdoing. Joseph's response was startling for someone who had suffered so much pain.

Joseph said, "God *sent me* before you to preserve life. . . . God *sent me* before you to preserve for you a remnant of earth, and to keep alive for you many survivors."[6] Joseph saw that even in the midst of the tragic circumstances of slavery and imprisonment, HaShem was with him and was using the circumstances to shape Joseph's life. Ultimately Joseph's tragic circumstances became the fulfillment of the purpose for which he was sent into the world.

Again, Joseph's story is not an exception to the way the Creator works; it is the pattern! Just as it was with Joseph in the midst of his tragedies, so it is with you. The fact that your life has caved in doesn't mean that the Creator is not working with and for you. The exact opposite is true. The Creator is shaping your life in the midst of the circumstances. It may take a while—Joseph sat in a dungeon for two years. The dungeon you are sitting in, whether physical, spiritual, or emotional, may be a dank, dark time, but that fact doesn't mean that you have been abandoned. The message that sings from Joseph is that the Creator is with you.

. . . The challenge becomes, can you be with the Creator?

I wonder how many times you have abandoned your goals and intentions because you became discouraged when things weren't happening fast enough. Impatience often impedes the cosmic power. Instead of abandoning a project, a desire, or an intention, what may be called for is to take the necessary steps to turn yourself in the same direction the Creator is moving.

The Ganges

The Ganges River is sacred to all Hindu people. It begins high in the Himalayas, then runs down across the northern plains of India, emptying into the Bay of Bengal. Each year literally millions of people come to its banks to bathe. They do so because the Ganges represents this power of the Tao, of the Holy Spirit, of the metaphorical stream described by Leslie Weatherhead. Inherent in the Ganges are the intentional, the circumstantial, and the ultimate will of the divine presence Hindus call Brahma.

Vatsala Sperling, in her marvelous children's book, *Ganga: The River that Flows from Heaven to Earth*, tells the story of how the Ganges was created. The Ganges is named after the goddess Ganga. When Ganga was a small child dwelling in the pantheon of the gods, she was known for her laughter and her sense of humor. However, the other gods did not always appreciate her antics. Once the strong wind of Pavan, the god of the wind, blew the robe off of Sage Durvasa, who had been walking through the heavens. The young Ganga laughed at his dilemma. Sage Durvasa was so angry that he cursed Ganga to become a river on earth. The young Ganga apologized for her wrongdoing and asked that the curse be lifted. Sage Durvasa believed that she was sincere but could not recall his curse. Instead he changed the curse to a blessing. Sage Durvasa said that people would come to her banks in their time of sorrows, and her waters would release them from pain and cleanse their brokenness.

When humans began calling to heaven to ask the gods to be with them in the hardships of life, Lord Brahma released Ganga. Her current was so strong that it began as a huge torrent. Lord Shiva was called upon to constrain and channel her power. As Ganga flowed through the land, everything she touched filled with abundant life. When Ganga touched the ashes of those who had died, their spirits were released. People began coming to Ganga not just to sit by her banks but to bathe and wash in her waters. Ganga cleansed people of their brokenness, pain, and sorrow as she brought them the power of Lords Brahma, Vishnu, and Shiva.[7]

The intentional will of Ganga was her joyful presence in the heavens with the pantheon of gods. The pain of her circumstances brought her to earth. However, Brahma, Vishnu, and Shiva did not abandon her; instead, their presence flowed through her. Ganga's circumstances mingled with the circumstances of the earth and flowed through the pain of humanity. People came to Ganga to find healing. Through Ganga they realize that Brahma is not absent from them, but is in their midst. As she empties into the Bay of Bengal, the ultimate purpose for Ganga is realized as she joins the vast oceans of all of creation.

When you feel as though your life has been broken, do you isolate yourself? Do you run into your room and pull the blinds? Do you abandon projects midcourse because things are not going your way? If so, then you miss the power of Ganga. As Hindus come to her banks to bathe and cleanse themselves, so must you. Maybe a plane ticket to India is too costly, but there are other ways to connect yourself with her power. You may simply go to the sink and turn on the faucet, or stand in the shower and allow the water to pour over your head. Take a tall glass and fill it with water and drink it down, to remind yourself of Ganga. Remind yourself that the power flowing through her water flows through you. The power of Brahma, Vishnu, and Shiva are within the banks of the Ganges, but symbolically they are with each draft of water you drink. The water can cleanse you and remind you that the power of the heavens is not distant but is right with you, flowing in the midst of your life. The next time it rains, go outside, lean your head back, and open your mouth. Allow each drop that touches your tongue to remind you that you are not alone. Brahma, Vishnu, and Shiva are with you. The Tao flows through you. The Holy Spirit fills you. The power of the Creator flows through your body like the blood in your veins. Do not give up on life; instead open yourself to possibilities that exceed your imagination.

Ask and Imagine

The epigraph for this chapter comes from the Christian New Testament, Ephesians 3:20: "*Now to him who by the power at work within us is able to accomplish abundantly far more than all we can ask or imagine.*" The key words are *ask* and *imagine*. These words align us with the movement of the Creator.

When was the last time you just sat back and imagined a new way of life? How often do you stop and visualize the fulfillment of your greatest dream? We encourage children and adolescents to imagine, yet we limit adults. People think that the older they become, the more their choices are limited. This type of thinking is how we misalign ourselves with the Creator's movement.

Try this: imagine what you have been sent you to do. Take a stab at it. Sit back and imagine what this could be. Don't hold back or limit yourself—imagine it, picture it. Ask the Cosmic Being to crank open your soul like a rusty trap door and free within you what you are supposed to do with your life. Let go of negative self-talk. Stop saying, "I'm too old, too poor, too young, too broke." Just imagine. When we ask and imagine, it aligns us with what the Creator is already doing.

Now, step beyond what you are asking and imagining. Consider that what you are picturing is too small for your life. Your divine purpose and desire are beyond all this. The power of the Creator pushes like the Ganges River. It flows beyond everything you could ask or imagine. The dungeons of your life cannot limit the movement of the Cosmic Being. The dark times of your soul do not keep its power from generating light. The challenge is to remain open. When you give up, abandon a desire, or turn away from what you are supposed to be doing, you run counter to its flow.

In the midst of life's dungeons you must summon the courage, creativity, and endurance to work with the Creator. If you find yourself in a dungeon, you need to believe that just as HaShem was with Joseph, so the Creator is with you, also. Joseph's story is the example of what the Hebrew psalmist says, "The Lord will fulfill his purpose for me."[8] The Creator has sent you with a dream, and you need to believe with your whole being that it will be realized. Don't hold back; dive into the Ganges. Allow the power of HaShem and the strength of Brahma, Vishnu, and Shiva to guide you.

If you can know in your being that the Creator is working with you, then you are empowered to actively choose to work with this force. Whatever your circumstances, you must use your free will and choose to collaborate with the Holy One. But this is where so many of us get lost, which is why we need to understand the essence of our free will.

Questions to Help You Discover and
Explore Your Divine Purpose

1. Were you born into fortunate or unfortunate circumstances? How was God present with you in the midst of your childhood?

2. What was the intentional will of God for your life before you were born? Did the first years of your life empower or hinder God's intentional will?

3. As you grew into an adolescent and young adult, how was God active through the circumstantial will? Did God raise up people to guide you? If so, who were they? What role did they play in your life? Would you say that God sent them to you?

4. What is the greatest crisis that has come into your adult life? Looking back, do you see that God was present with you during these circumstances? How was God present to you during this time? How did God feel absent from you?

5. What do you imagine God's ultimate will for your life to look like?

Love, tell an incident
That will clarify this mystery
of how we act freely
And are yet compelled.

—Rumi

Chapter Three

The Holy Hairball

F ree will is a holy hairball. We are given the choice to fulfill our destiny or ignore it. It's hard to imagine why the Creator gave us free will. If our destiny provides meaning, hope, and a sense of purpose, why would we have the option to choose not to do this? If some significant aspect of the planet's future hangs on our ability to fulfill our destiny, it only makes sense that we would not have the option to refuse. But it's a part of the creation. Like it or not, blessing or curse, it's ours to choose how we are going to live.

For many people free will is a curse. They make one poor choice after another and their lives sink into misery. The Buddha taught a *jataka*[1] about such a person from one of his early incarnations— about a young, foolish king, Upakara.

It was at a time when the earth was young and the people naïve. King Upakara told a young servant that he was going to tell a lie so that the servant could become his chief advisor. On the appointed day when King Upakara was going to lie, a huge crowd gathered. Among those in the crowd was the sage Kapila. Before Upakara opened his mouth, Kapila warned the king of the dire effects that a lie could have and that Upakara would sink into the ground until he ended in hell. The king ignored Kapila and uttered his lie. The town's people stood aghast as their king sank in the dirt to his ankles. The wise sage Kapila warned the king to think about what he was going to say next, and to choose his words wisely. The king lied again and sank to his knees. Once again, Kapila urged the king to be thoughtful and to choose to tell the truth. He lied a third time and sank to his navel. A fourth and fifth time the sage urged the king to be thoughtful. If Upakara chose to tell the truth, he could reverse the sinking process and step into abundant life. The sixth time the king lied, his choices doomed him, and with his last words he slipped beneath the soil and sank into the depths of darkness.[2] At the close of the story the Buddha said that in this past incarnation he was Kapila and his foolish student was Upakara.

The story conveys the tension of the effect our choices have. If you fail to understand the impact of your decisions, then you are like King Upakara. Choose poorly and you sink into the mire of existence; choose rightly, however, and you have the ability to shine with opportunity. With each decision, though, there is the Buddha inviting you to think and reflect upon the choice you are about to make.

This is one of the great blessings that Buddhism brings to the world. Buddhism invites us to think and live intentionally. Shakyamuni, the Buddha, provided the balance between insight and action. On one hand he provided the spiritual guidance that led to enlightenment. On the other were the clear steps to engage the path. The Four Noble Truths are spiritual insights: life is full of suffering; our suffering is caused by our wants and desires; there is a way out of our suffering; the way is the Eightfold Path. The Eightfold Path consists of intentional practices, choices a person makes. Like the sage Kapila, the Buddha provides insight. Like Upakara, we listen and then choose how to live. The Four Noble Truths are indeed that: truth. But if we choose a life devoid of compassion, then we choose a path that will cause us to sink into suffering. Right actions lead to enlightenment. Wrong actions stir the dirt of a person's soul. It's a choice.

The human ability to choose lies at the heart of the Abrahamic faiths. The Jewish scriptures are filled with stories of choices and their consequences. HaShem creates Adam and Eve and places them within the Garden of Eden. He commands them not to eat of the tree of the knowledge of good and evil. Yet, they *choose* to do so. Sure, they are tempted, but it is their own action, their own free will, that allows them to go against the divine command. If Adam and Eve had lived in a predetermined system, then HaShem's command would have restricted their actions. But it's the exact opposite. They are placed in the garden and given a command that leaves them the option of not fulfilling HaShem's wishes.

The very next story, of Cain and Abel, is an expression of free will. Cain and Abel both make offerings to HaShem. Abel's offering is accepted and Cain's is rejected. Cain is angry and jealous and can choose how he will act. If he were fated to kill his brother, HaShem would have said, "Sorry, I just like Abel better than you. I created you to be second fiddle. By the way, you're about to do something horrendous. You're going to kill your brother. I will judge you as a murderer and condemn you forever. Welcome to your life."

Does this sound like a Divine Being that you know and love?

I don't think so either.

Cain wrestled with his decision and chose to kill his brother Abel. He wasn't forced, fated, or determined. He chose to pick up a hammer and kill his brother in the field. When HaShem discovered what Cain had done, he was shocked and dismayed.

The characters in the Jewish scriptures are presented with the ability to choose and then forced to deal with the consequences. David chooses to have an affair with Bathsheba and to kill her husband, Uriah the Hittite, so that he can marry her. David laments and grieves his wrong-headed choices. The implications are terrifying. If HaShem didn't stop King David, one of the heroes of the faith, from exercising his free will, then you won't be stopped either. If you are bound and determined to destroy your life, then guess what—you can. You are blessed with free will, and the Creator expects you to use it.

In the Christian scriptures, Jesus, up until the moment of his death, has free will. While he is praying in the Garden of Gethsemane he wrestles with the options set before him. He knows he doesn't have to go through the ordeal that is waiting for him. He can take the disciples and run for the countryside, away from Jerusalem. Jesus's prayer gets at the heart of the dilemma of free will: "Yet not what I want but what you want."[3]

Free will is central to the teachings of Islam. While Allah's will is all-powerful, the individual Muslim is free to express his or her own desires within the scope of Allah's creation. "Then whosoever wills, let him believe, and whosoever wills, let him disbelieve."[4]

The entire teaching of the Bhagavad Gita assumes an individual's ability to choose. The book begins with time suspended as Arjuna and Krishna, standing at the edge of a great battle, discuss how Arjuna should respond. Arjuna is unsure whether he should enter into battle against his kinsmen. Krishna's response is the Bhagavad Gita. The book ends with Arjuna turning his attention from Krishna back to the battle before him. His concluding words are a reflection of his free will. He could have chosen to retreat with his troops, but he chooses differently. He chooses to respond as Krishna has taught: "I will *act* according to your command."

While there are great disagreements among the world's faiths, they share the common ground that you were born with the freedom to choose. While your past karma may have brought you to this place in time, it's up to you to decide. Whether you believe in just one life or in a past life, there are no excuses for what happens next. As the bumper sticker says, "If you want to predict the future, there's no better way than to create it."

The Pregnant Moment

I like the phrase *pregnant with possibilities*.[5] Have you ever seen a pregnant woman in the last weeks before she delivers? Her belly is as taut as a party balloon. Everyone around her is filled with anticipation because they know that at any moment she's going to pop. It is an apocalyptic moment; people are on edge because they know a wondrous event is coming. Each second of our lives is filled with this same kind of potential.

As the clock ticks, a moment expands until it is full and ripe. What gives birth to the moment are our choices. While the Creator cast us into the world with intention and is active in our circumstances, the Cosmic Being has to wait on our choices.

Let's say that you come home from a day at work and have a few extra hours to kill. You can choose to do a myriad of different things. You can choose to exercise your free will by munching popcorn in front of the television. The Creator honors that choice but is not satisfied. It will work like crazy to prick your conscience to move you in a positive direction. But if you choose the television, the one who created you has no option but to step aside.

Once I sat beside a woman who was dying in a hospice. After her lifelong addiction to smoking, black crud was being drained from her lungs like tar being dumped from a truck. She sucked on a cigarette as oxygen was pumped into her nose (apparently oblivious to the fact that, with one stray ash, both she and I might detonate). She was furious. "Why is God doing this to me?" she ranted. I had to bite my tongue and listen patiently. The Creator honored her choice to smoke.

Let's go back to our evening of possibilities. If you come home and choose to be creative, to work, to be active, to seek out and discern why you were sent into the world, then the Creator actively engages you. If you choose to attend night classes, to do homework, to practice, to listen, to read, then the cosmic force is as active as your free will allows.

Roger's life caved in on him. Like King Upakara he made one terrible decision after another that sank his life into despair. He had an affair that ruined his marriage. His wife left him, and he overextended himself financially, living on credit cards. During an economic downturn he was laid off. Roger filed for bankruptcy and lost his home, his car, and his family. When he came to see me he settled into his chair like a rumpled pile of laundry. Tears rolled down his cheeks, tiny rivers of pain, as he shared his desire to end his life. He was at rock bottom.

Over a series of conversations we talked about the grace and mercy of the Creator. That rumpled pile of laundry became a bit smoother. We talked about the choices that he had made in his life and the choices that were now before him. I shared my belief that he had been sent into the world for a sacred destiny, and I asked Roger if he knew what his purpose was. I was startled when he clearly explained that he knew why he had been sent, but he had chosen not to fulfill that purpose.

I wondered silently, "Why, if you knew, were you not acting on it?" Roger said that for years he had felt that he was sent to use his skills in the helping professions. He had gone to college, though, to be an engineer. It was only after marriage and kids that he realized that his heart and skills lay in other places. As an engineer he felt like a fish out of water, but he felt stuck by all the responsibilities of raising a family. To cover his dissatisfaction, he chose to do things that undermined his health and well-being.

As we talked, Roger began to realize that he could start making different choices at any moment. Roger was not predetermined to live a miserable life—he could use his free will to send his life in a different direction. Roger, at the age forty-eight, made the choice to earn a degree, fulfilling the reason he had been sent. Roger realized that the Creator had given him a "say-so."[6]

You are given a say-so in determining your life by the gift of free will. It's not complete autonomy, but it is a say-so. You get to chime in, influence, and choose the direction your life takes. You can also neglect, abuse, and refuse. But you always have the ability to dialogue with the Creator. You are invited to be a co-creator.

Use It and Choose It

While we do have free will, and we are given a say-so, the Ultimate Being hopes we will choose those things that further the sacred intentions for our lives. There is a divine bias.

Think about your own life. Most of the time you have a preference regarding the way you want things to turn out. Imagine you are going out with friends for dinner and a movie. You love being with these people and you are open to almost anything that they want to do . . . unless it's Chinese food for dinner. While you really like Chinese, you've been eating it for the last couple of nights. This evening you prefer Italian, Mexican, almost anything but Chinese. But if this is what they choose, then, what the heck, you'll go along, but you *do have a preference.*

It's the same with the Creator. You were given free will with the expectation that you will "use it and choose it." You were given a say-so in directing your life with the expectation that you would do exactly that—choose a direction.

However, there is a sacred bias toward decisions that fulfill your divine purpose. Additionally, the Cosmic Being has a bias for compassion, justice, and love. If your choice will be self-destructive or oppressive to other people, clearly this is not the direction that you were sent.

Trials and tragedies present the greatest challenges, and when faced with them we struggle to ask, "Where is God now?" How can I choose for God even now, surrounded by pain?"

Evan was devastated when he was diagnosed with a stage four glioblastoma brain tumor. He was an active young man in his twenties and was relishing his freedom as a young adult. The tumor and the chemotherapy bulldozed through his life like a tank. At first Evan was bitter and angry. But through his chemotherapy treatments he began to meet other young people with tumors and cancers.

While staying at a Ronald McDonald house, he was inspired by the ways children and families dealt with their illnesses, with hope and happiness. He marveled at how they could be optimistic in the face of death. Evan began to realize that there was a "divine presence" with them, even as they battled cancer. In dealing with his own cancer, Evan could have chosen to face his future with an overwhelming sense of doom and gloom, or he could use his circumstances as an opportunity to reach out to others. Evan chose to use his illness to work to inspire other patients to live with joy and optimism.

It all comes down to choice. You have free will. The religions of the world teach that you are radically free and the Creator waits for you to act. I still say free will is the hairball in creation. It was either the most brilliant divine act or one that was not completely thought through.

The Creator has gone to all the trouble to preknow us, endow us with gifts, and send us into the creation, only to also plant within us the ability to short-wire the whole shebang. It just doesn't make sense. Why would the Cosmic Being give us the ability to choose not to fulfill our destiny? You would think that if we were sent to fulfill a sacred purpose we would simply have no choice. We would grow up knowing deep within ourselves what we were supposed to do. Our gifts would develop and mature. Through childhood, adolescence, and young adulthood we would benefit from the care and guidance of others who made sure we received the right training and education to empower the divine plan. Then bingo, off we would go, running like playful puppies, fulfilling our destinies. Why risk the whole design by giving us a choice? Free will has injected a dynamic that keeps the whole creation on edge wondering if, when, and how we are going to finally get off our spiritual backsides.

Fortunately, the world is full of people who actively work to discover the holy purpose of their lives. They are constantly hunting for the reason they were sent into the world. They never tire of new ideas and insights. They assess their gifts and constantly hone their abilities. Once they have discovered their divine dream they commit themselves body and soul. They make sacrifices so that their destiny might live and flourish.

When people choose for the divine bias, often doors fly open as if they were on greased hinges. People suddenly appear who provide inspiration and guidance. But it's not just coincidence; people who choose to activate their sacred purpose are also intentionally seeking others to guide them.

Julie Pech is truly an entrepreneur. She is a successful businesswoman, public speaker, and author. Her charisma is infectious, but she has also had more than her fair share of troubles. She knew that she had a choice in how she was going to live. Julie knew that she had been sent to this planet for a reason, and she was determined to discover what it was.

Julie realized many years ago that while she had great business skills, the Creator wanted her to do more than make money. She sought outside guidance from people she respected and admired.

CHAPTER THREE

She took risks, personally and financially, that kept her on a spiritual edge. Each day Julie chose to cocreate with the Ultimate Being.

In addition to running a thriving business, Julie speaks to women all over the world to inspire them. When speaking, she is keenly aware that she is not alone, that a divine presence is with her. Julie will tell you that it's a choice. She has to choose each day to discover her purpose and fulfill her destiny.

The Cosmic Being takes a tremendous risk by giving you free will. The entire future of your life, and possibly the future of the planet, rests on the choices you make. This is why free will is a holy hairball. But the risk also has a huge payoff. If you choose to discover your destiny, align yourself with your divine purpose, and live that purpose each day, the abundance of the heavens is expressed through you. Through your choices, the love and mercy of the Creator flows to those who are hurting in the world. This whole design is a huge cosmic gamble. The question becomes . . .

Are you worthy of such a gamble?

You have been given life, but it really is your choice. Use it and choose it. You have a say-so in what happens to you. So, what will you say? "Give me some more pretzels and a beer while I zone out in front of the tube"? If so, then move over one cushion and allow King Upakara to join you. Together you can slip into oblivion one pretzel at a time.

There is another choice though. As the Dalai Lama taught, "Think critically, act accordingly."[7] As you sit on the couch ask yourself, "How can I use this night, this day, this moment, to take the next step toward fulfilling the reason I was sent into the world?"

Questions to Help You Discover and
Explore Your Divine Purpose

1. Do you believe that you live in a mechanistic world? Were you predetermined? Explain your answers.

2. Do you agree with the fatalistic worldview, which says that you have no ability to influence what happens to you? If so, how does a book like this challenge your thinking? If you do not agree, how do you account for the accidents that occur in life? Are these accidents sent to us by God?

3. What do you believe about free will? Do you have free will? How have you exercised your free will?

4. What are some of the hardest choices that you have made in your life? Did God influence any of your choices? If so, how?

5. What are some choices that you have made that have been detrimental to your life?

6. How do you understand God's omnipotence and your free will? Does God's power ever eclipse your ability to choose?

7. Does God ever override the decisions you have made? If so, provide some examples.

The arrow is the intention that leaves the archer's hand
And sets off toward the target,
That is, it is free in its flight and will follow
The path chosen for it when released.

—Paul Coelho

Chapter Four

The Divine Archer

Y ou make a mistake when you think you only have one life purpose. The Cosmic Being is more dynamic and much too creative to have just one plan. I believe there are *plans* for your life.

It's like going on a camping trip with your family. Your plan is to go from Los Angeles to Yellowstone. So you pack the trailer with tents, stove, and coolers of food and beer, load the kids and the dog into the Dodge minivan, and hit the road. You have carefully planned the journey. You map out your trip to stop in Provo for the first night and stay in a Motel 8. Day two is Yellowstone. You're set for a great two-week vacation. Things are going fine—the kids are watching one DVD after another and the dog is asleep—then somewhere outside Cedar City, Utah, you blow a radiator hose.

You pull over and pop the hood, and steam billows out as if you were boiling crabs. Now what are you going to do? Luckily you have OnStar, which I think is an amazing "God thing" installed in cars. You push a button and a calm voice says from the speaker, "OnStar, how can I help?" How cool is that? In the middle of your crisis, out in the middle of nowhere OnStar comes to the rescue. Wouldn't it be nice to have this kind of on-the-spot assistance built not only into our cars, but into our brains as well?

Imagine you hit some sort of crisis in your life. You have been laid off. You need a job fast, ideally before you get home and tell your spouse.

CHAPTER FOUR

So you push on the side of your temple, and the voice of the Cosmic Being echoes in your head, "GodStar, may I help you?" "Yeah, I need a job, and fast. I've just been laid off. It'd be great if I could have it all lined up before I walk in the front door. My spouse has been a little edgy lately and I could use some security."

"No problem," says the divine voice. "I have you at the corner of Washington and Brant streets. You have a few choices here: Do you want to stay with sales, or do you want to make a radical switch and go back to nursing school? If it's sales, turn left on Washington and go to Gates Engineering. They have a job that matches your skills; actually it would be a step up in pay and security. If you want nursing, call your community college. Their nursing program is fantastic. I'm doing some of my best work through their graduates.

"While you may think this is crazy, I put this idea in your brain when you were with me long ago. You've always thought about becoming a nurse, but you opted for sales instead, which was also in the plans. Either option was fine with me, as were endless other possibilities. To pay the bills while you go back to school, you may have to work graveyard at the Gas-n-Go—I have that option in the wings if you need it. You may also need to sell your car and eat hotdogs for a year. This sounds like a huge sacrifice, but you'll thank me when you get the job in the neonatal ICU. They will be hiring in one year—trust me, I know these things. Every day you'll come home exhausted but deeply satisfied that you're serving those little lives. Personally, I hope you choose nursing; it's my bias for you. It fits you better than sales, but really, it's your choice. I'm with you either way."

The GodStar voice fades out and you are faced with a choice. Again, it's all about choices. Plans change, whether you have been laid off or you've blown a radiator hose. The challenge is to be creative and make a choice.

But back to our family stuck in the desert. OnStar tells you that a tow truck has been dispatched and will be there in an hour. "Great," you think. At least you won't be stuck. But now what do you do? What are your options?

Well, you want to stay with your vacation plans. But the mechanic says it will cost seven hundred dollars to fix your car and it won't be ready for three days. What are you going to do? Well, you could choose to sit and mope. You could rent a cheap motel room and waste your time. Or you could be creative and change your plans.

You buy the kids some ice cream and you break out the map with your spouse. "Look at this!" you say. "Bryce and Zion National Parks are only an hour-and-half drive from Cedar City." You could rent a car, hook up the trailer, and see both parks while a mechanic fixes the Dodge. You're flexible, creative, you think outside your box, and suddenly you have new plans—a vacation in two national parks *and* a new radiator! Life is good. You can be this creative, and so can the Cosmic Being. A sacred dynamic force works through the circumstances of your life.

Stochastic Craziness

I like the term *stochastic process* to describe the Creator's plans. *Stochastic*, from the Greek word *stokos*, means "aiming" or "guessing" and occurs in the midst of unpredictability. While there may be an initial intention for your life, as it unfolds and interacts with the environment, it's really anybody's guess as to what is going to happen next.

A stochastic process is like an archer shooting an arrow. Pulling back the bow, the archer has an *original intention*, an *initial aim*. But when the arrow is released no one knows where it will land.

The arrow encounters all types of environmental factors. Winds buffet the arrow and move it off course. Rains hammer it and send it dipping below its target. A pigeon flies into the path of the arrow, gets hit right in the heart, and both arrow and pigeon tumble to the ground. In spite of the archer's original aim, the manner in which the arrow interacts with the environment is what really determines its final destination.

Your camping trip from Los Angeles to Yellowstone was a stochastic process. Your original intent was to see Old Faithful and the park bears. You had a plan; you were the archer. When you packed the car the night before the trip, you pulled back on the bow. As you drove down the driveway and entered the highway, you released the arrow.

You made your plan but it was actually a very random process. On the way to Yellowstone you interacted with the environment around you. You had to contend with the mess of L.A. traffic. You had the desert heat, and eventually your radiator hose blew, which was akin to the arrow hitting the pigeon.

As your trip unfolded, your plan continually changed. You had to decide how to interact with each situation. When your car broke down you could have chosen to sell the Dodge and buy a plane ticket to Copenhagen. What you thought was a predetermined route held countless random possibilities.

As you check in with the Creator, you begin to realize that your life, too, is filled with countless random possibilities. Whatever path you choose has a whole different set of possibilities. Again it's all about creativity, choices, and seeking the divine bias in the midst of life.

A stochastic process is at the heart of the way you were sent. Let's make the Cosmic Being the archer and you the arrow. Before you were born, the Creator held the divine goo that was to become you and planted a purpose and intention that held countless possibilities. Then there was a grand pull on the bowstring of life.

At the moment of your conception, the arrow was released and you were sent into the creation. From that instant on, you began interacting with a myriad of environmental factors, many that you could not control. As an embryo, you have no control over whether your mother is a crack addict or an alcoholic. Your little embryo arrow flying through the amniotic fluid depends completely on the choices she makes. But your little embryo is not alone, for even at this stage, the circumstantial will of the Creator acts to further the sacred intentions for your life.

Some wonder at this point about the ethical issues of artificial insemination, in which multiple eggs are fertilized and harvested but only a few eggs are implanted. What happens to the divine will of those destroyed embryos? Is this an example of doctors playing God, creating and then destroying life? Others use this as an argument against stem cell research or abortion. If the power of the Cosmic Being is present within the fertilized cells, should they be disturbed?

These concerns, while serious ethical issues, do not thwart the divine power that is present within each moment. The fact that a doctor harvests, fertilizes, and implants an egg does not discount that the Creator is working through that doctor and the choices made. Remember, the OB-GYN was sent for a holy purpose as well. The doctor must wrestle with his or her "say-so" in ethical ways that reflect a divine bias. While an embryo has no voice in the decision, the will of the Creator is working intentionally, circumstantially, and ultimately. The demise of a fertilized egg is no different from the demise of a ninety-year-old adult. Both lives are taken into the ultimate will—the reunion with the Cosmic Being. These issues, while weighty and in many ways beyond the scope of this book, reflect the stochastic process of being sent. A myriad of possibilities are present.

When the arrow of your life develops from an embryo to a newborn, the random nature of the divine plan becomes even more chaotic because you are now interacting with a countless number of possibilities. Are you born in a hospital with doctors and nurses, or are you born in a refugee village on the outskirts of a war zone? The environment into which you are born directly affects the flight of your arrow. But again, you are not alone—the divine circumstantial will, like the mighty Ganges, is advocating, interacting, and moving mountains to further your purpose.

As you grow from adolescence into young adulthood, the divine purpose begins to emerge. You become aware of your gifts and abilities. A deep desire for what you want to do as an adult develops. You realize that you have certain passions that differ greatly from others. The circumstantial will becomes very active as teachers, mentors, and friends are raised up to guide and shape you.

The natural environment dramatically impacts the way in which the divine intentions unfold in your life. Maybe you were born in an area prone to tornados, and when you were a teenager one ripped into your house, lifting the roof like the lid off a can of beans. The path of the tornado is a random stochastic process that destroys one house and leaves another untouched. Cancer, MS, diabetes, Alzheimer's, and AIDs—diseases are not sent into the world as divine punishment; they are part of the random nature of the environment. But if you experience tragedies, you are not alone; the circumstantial will is very active, drawing people to your aid. Your tragedy interacts with the purpose of other people's lives, and together you and they work to realize your divine potential.

Aiming Your Own Arrow

Your free will to choose is the hairball of this stochastic process and really sends things flying in crazy directions. The Creator needs you to take an active role in the way your life unfolds. Every choice you make dramatically affects your arrow's flight. Your life can be aimed, but the ultimate destination is a random stochastic process that interacts with a countless number of variables. While you have been sent, this fact does not mean your life has a rigid, predetermined destiny. The Creator of the cosmos doesn't have a dream for you—it has *dreams* for you.

As you choose and interact with the crazy nature of the world, the Creator responds to your choices. Like the divine OnStar in your brain, you are continually presented with different options; you can continue to be an engineer, or you can go into nursing or firefighting. Any way you choose, the Cosmic Being remains present with you, acting and advocating on your behalf.

However, as you choose, the challenge is to always be mindful of the divine bias for your life. You may choose to be a day-care provider, but if your gift is to work as a forest ranger, your choice stifles you. You will feel unsettled and unfulfilled. The circumstantial will pushes at your soul like the tide of the Ganges. You will know deep within yourself that you are wasting your time, that your gifts are not being used. This is not to discount those who work with children. The analogy also works conversely: if you're wandering through Yellowstone feeling lonely and frustrated because you long to work with preschoolers, then you too will feel the circumstantial will burning in your soul. You will feel satisfied only if you make the necessary changes in your life.

The Turd Herder

I had a conversation with a city manager who argued with my basic premise that we have been sent. He told me about his sanitation supervisor, Jim. When the manager asks Jim how he's doing, Jim always replies, "Just another day herding turds." The manager implored, "Don't tell me God sent Jim into the world to run the sewage plant!" I asked, "Is Jim satisfied with his work? Does he find meaning herding turds?" The manager told me that Jim loves his job and is a dedicated employee. Then more than likely Jim is fulfilling his divine destiny.

The fact that someone's job involves things that we may not like, don't have an interest in, or may find hard to stomach, doesn't mean that they have not been sent. Thank God Jim was sent into the world. The world needs people who can herd turds in the right direction. We would all be up the creek without a paddle if there weren't people like Jim.

Being sent doesn't mean we are all going to win Nobel Prizes, write Pulitzer Prize–winning novels, or be recognized as citizens of the year. We have been sent to fulfill a myriad of destinies. None is greater than any other. The Creator has sent turd herders, cow herders, child herders, and on and on. The challenges you confront and the gifts you have enable you to aim your arrow so that your choices reflect the divine trajectory.

As you live in the midst of crises and opportunities you have to actively think, "What bias does the Creator have for me right now? How can I act to realize the divine potential in this moment?" In a given situation there are literally thousands of ways to respond, but only a few reflect a sacred trajectory.

Choices, choices, choices—each moment of your life is filled with choices. The Divine Being lures, pleads, and urges you to make certain decisions, but ultimately it's up to you to choose.

Think right now about the flight of your life. Is it your destiny to camp in Yellowstone? If so, are you making the right choices to get there? Are you standing at the corner of Washington and Brant feeling confused about which direction to go? Are you waiting for GodStar to tell you? If you are, then you need to open up your third eye of discernment and pay attention, because GodStar is there. It's not an illusion. GodStar may be a silly metaphor, but the voice of the Creator is speaking to you, yelling to you even, that you are supposed to be doing something significant with your life! Can you hear this holy voice humming within you, or are you deaf to its song? Discerning the sacred muse is very simple. You need to learn how to ask and answer five basic questions.

Questions to Help You Discover and Explore Your Divine Purpose

1. What are the different paths that the arrow of your life has taken?

2. What obstacles has the arrow of your life encountered?

3. What choices have you made that have furthered or hindered the flight of your arrow?

4. Was there a time in your life when you felt that God's purpose in sending you into the world was realized? Describe it.

It's as if a King has sent you to some country to do a task, and you
Perform a hundred other services, but not the one he sent you to do.
So human beings come to this world to do particular work. That
    work is the purpose,
And each is specific to the person. If you'd not do it, it's as though a
    priceless Indian sword
Were used to slice rotten meat.

—Rumi

Chapter Five

The Divine Convergence

It comes as an epiphany, an "ah-ha," a great thunderbolt of understanding for some, or the dawning of an idea for others. I call it "the Divine Convergence." When you learn how to ask and answer five basic questions, the forces of the cosmos converge, leading you to understand your dharma.

Dharma is Sanskrit for "deep, deep integrity, living by your inner truth."[1] Brahman planted dharma within you as a soul code holding the DNA of what you are supposed to do in life. The power of embodying your dharma provides a one-to-one relationship with Brahman. You are doing exactly what the magnificent God sent you to do. The distinction between body and soul evaporates as you live each day constantly in the presence of the Holy One.

The goal of all the world religions is to bring you into complete union with the Creator as you name it: Brahman, Tao, God, Allah, HaShem, Emptiness, the Cosmos. While each religion proposes a different path for attaining this union, the common bond between them is a profound sense of identity found when we discover and embody our sacred purpose for life. The vision quest was central to many Native American tribes. A young boy was sent out on a solo journey to meditate and wait for Wakan Tanka to reveal his life purpose.[2] When he received the vision, he lived in complete unity with the Creator—there was no separation. His vision was his dharma realized. It was the movement of the Tao embodied. It was the presence of the Holy Spirit in his life. He was one with the Creator. The same oneness is readily available to you.

When you wrestle with five key questions, eventually an internal epiphany dawns as to what your dharma is. This is why I strongly encourage you to work your way through the questions at the end of each chapter. The questions are designed to help you wrestle with these topics to discover your dharma.

These five key questions lead to the divine convergence: What are my passions? What are my joys? What are my fears? What is my anger? What are my gifts? As you spend time thinking through your answers, your ideas will mesh. There will be a whirl of thoughts revealing deep and profound insights. Your divine destiny will swim up out of the depths of your heart. Let's look at each of these questions individually.

What Are Your Passions?

What are you passionate about? What wakes you up in the morning before the alarm because you are excited about getting after it? What keeps you up at night thinking and planning? What books and magazines fuel your excitement? What do you daydream about? What do you aspire to? As a child what did you want to be when you grew up? What do you want to be when you *grow up* now? Even if you are sixty-five or seventy-five, you likely still have that childlike desire to "be" something. What is it that, when you start talking about it, you just can't shut up? All of these questions are hints about your passions.

The Creator did not send us into the world to work and live for something we are not passionate about. But I don't want to confuse working to make a living with working to fulfill a passion. We often earn a paycheck doing work that is separate from our passions.

John is passionate about martial arts but makes his living as an engineer. He is tremendously gifted in designing buildings and gas lines. However, his imagination sparks when he talks about martial arts. He loves the tradition, the physical movement, the exercise, and the development of physical power. He earns a paycheck as an engineer, but when he opened a martial arts school for people of all ages, his heart began to soar. When he steps through the doors of his *dojang*, he immediately feels he has stepped into his divine purpose.[3] John realized early in his involvement with martial arts that he had a knack for teaching them, especially to kids with physical, mental, and emotional challenges. These kids find a loving, accepting place in John's school.

For John, martial arts are the avenue by which the Creator works to empower these young lives. He loves to encourage children and cheer them on. He has the patience of Job, working step-by-step with each child. John earns a paycheck as an engineer, but martial arts are his passion and his heart soars when he is in a dojang working with kids.

It's a great gift when we can earn a living doing what we are passionate about. However, we have to sometimes hold our passions in tension with the need for an income. Ideally, the two are one and the same. John's example shows how to hold the two in balance; however, even for John it can be a constant struggle. When his life becomes consumed by his engineering, pushing out the time for his passion, he feels stifled and frustrated.

When you stand at a crossroads, when you feel torn between many different possibilities, always ask yourself, "What am I passionate about? If I go down this path will my passions be fueled and fulfilled?" If the answer is no, then don't go another step in that direction. If you're not doing something you're passionate about, you will feel bored and frustrated. You will be wasting the precious life that the Creator has sent to you to unleash.

Remember, your passions are a direct link back to the original intentions for your life. If you stifle your passions, you are snuffing out the spark of the divine fire in your soul. Instead, you should be waving as much energy as possible over these embers until they burn hot within you.

What Are Your Joys?

"What's my joy?" I take Jesus seriously when he said his intended purpose was to bring us joy: "I have said these things to you so that my joy may be in you, and that your joy may be complete."[4] The Hindu Upanishads[5] teach that the purpose of our union with Brahman is to bring us complete joy. The Taittiriya Upanishad invites us to imagine a young person who is "healthy, strong, good, and cultured, who has all the wealth that earth can offer" and to take just one measure of his joy.[6] Then take this joy and multiply it one hundred times. This compounded joy is but one measure of all those who serve in the heavenly pantheon: the Gandharvas, the Pitrs, the Devas, the Karmadevas, Indra, Virat, and Prajapati.[7] The Upanishad teaches that this great joy, a wealth hundreds of times greater than that of the wealthiest person on earth, is possible for any human who realizes the fullness of Brahman. It is the divine intention to fill us with joy.

Your purpose is going to unfold around joy. So you need to constantly ask, "What brings me joy? What makes my heart sing? What makes me open up and want to be alive?" You were not sent to do something that dries up your soul. Like your passions, you need to constantly ask yourself, "Where's my joy?" If what you are doing doesn't bring you any joy, why are you doing it?

I find angry Christians a divine turnoff. There is a lot of truth in the bumper sticker, "I like Jesus, but his fan club scares me." I find the same is true with people of all faiths. Angry Muslims, unhappy Buddhists, hypercritical Hindus—all of these people devour themselves and each other with their negativity. They are toxic people who do not bear witness to the joy the Creator desires to bring into people's lives. I fear that people look at angry, judgmental people of faith and ask, "Why would I want to develop a relationship with the Ultimate Being if I'm going to end up acting like these negative people?"

There is a sacred space in the center of your chest. Your heart chakra lies right over your sternum.[8] It is the divine dwelling place in your body. When you find your joy, the heart chakra opens like a pathway to your soul. Your whole body rings with happiness when you are doing whatever fills you with joy.

What makes your heart open up? Does your heart sing when you are in the middle of a sales meeting? How about when you are framing a house? Does your heart thump when you are cradling a child, teaching math, or walking in the woods? There is no grander feeling than having your heart blossom in the midst of doing what brings you joy.

What is curious is how many people are completely out of touch with their joy. When working with groups I ask them, "What brings you joy?" I'm often met with blank stares—people just are not aware. When we do some brainstorming and people finally come to understand what brings them joy I ask them, "When was the last time you did this?" I'm dumbstruck when people tell me that it has been months, even years, since they have done what their heart longs for. It's no wonder people's souls feel like a dried-up sponge. When you fill your life with joy, it's like sinking that sponge into a well of deep, cool water. Your soul expands with the abundance of this bliss.

A wonderful part of joy comes when you join others who share your delight. Like passions, joy is something that cannot be contained. It is a communal affair. Whereas a passion is often an individual pursuit, your joy is compounded when you celebrate with others. A huge vibration moves through a crowd of people who share the same delight. Think of a football stadium that is rocking with energy because eighty thousand people have gathered together. Picture the intensity of laboratory technicians who celebrate new scientific breakthroughs.

The Creator sent you into the world to do something that makes your heart smile—not the opposite. Along with your passions, you need to clearly identify your joys. If Jesus came to bring you joy, if Brahman invites you to have an abundance of joy, and you ignore it, then you are turning down the great intention of the Divine Being.

What Are Your Fears?

It sounds like a silly question: "What are you afraid of?" As adults, we rarely give voice to our fears. Somewhere in our maturation we no longer give ourselves permission to name our fears. Sure, we can say offhandedly that we are afraid of heights or claustrophobic elevators, but I'm talking about something deeper. The fears I help people confront are the dark shadows that hover in the basements of their souls. If we can't clearly name these fears, they become silent impediments inhibiting our ability to courageously choose our divine destinies.

People fear four main things. It all boils down to death, money, looking like a fool, and loneliness.

Death

People are gripped by the fear of dying. Most of the time people can ignore this fear. They pretend they won't die for years. They tell themselves to live for the moment and forget about dying. They fool themselves into thinking that somehow they will not die; they will mysteriously just leave earth and appear in heaven. If this is what you are thinking, then I have news for you—it doesn't happen this way. There is no avoiding or getting around it. You are going to die and when you do, it will be grim. As a pastor for thirty years I have seen a lot of people die. I have learned that when you die it will be painful, bloody, and at times full of sheer panic. You may dodge this bullet by having the great blessing of dying suddenly from an aneurism, a heart attack, or a massive stroke; it will be "lights out" and "Hi Krishna!" It's too bad that only a few of us get to go out this way. I have known only five people who have died instantly.

Most people die only after moments, hours, maybe even days of sheer panic. You may have to endure the moments before a plane crash, the panic of feeling your life slipping away after a car wreck, or the hours of being stranded somewhere, injured and waiting for help. You may die a long death in which some illness hacks and whittles away your body until you're nothing. Medical books are full of descriptions of these ugly deaths.

You are going to die. Face it. However, one of the great gifts that come from building a relationship with the Ultimate Being is knowing that you are never abandoned in death; the Creator is constantly present with you. While every death I have attended was hard and painful, the one great constant that brought peace was that I knew that we were not alone. I have felt hospital rooms swell with the presence of angels. I have felt the breath of the Creator on the side of the road while I held a man as he died after crashing his

Harley head-on into a Corolla. A divine holy presence has filled bedrooms, battlefields, wilderness areas—any place people die, God's presence is there. I know it; I have felt it, as have thousands of others who work with death and dying.

For the Supreme Being, death is not a tragedy; instead it is our most profound teacher. In the Katha Upanishad, Yama, the King of Death, is the great instructor of the spiritual seeker Nachiketa. Death guides Nachiketa as he asks questions about meaning and life. Death brings clarity to Nachiketa, teaching that life's highest priority is to know Brahman and attain unity with him. The Katha Upanishad teaches that death is not something to run from, but something to turn to and from which to learn. Yama can be your great guide as you discern the reason you have been sent.

Too often we push away from what we have been sent to do because we are afraid that it might lead to our death. Let's be honest, this could happen to you. You may have been sent into the world for a purpose that puts your life at risk. If you have been sent to serve in the military, as a policeman, a refugee doctor, an activist in a violent place, then your risk of death dramatically increases in comparison with someone who has been sent to sit at a computer and write a book. I teach people to overcome their fear of death by contemplating the three deaths of their dying.[9]

The Grim Whittler. Our first death comes in the midst of our lives. We actually choose to die bit by bit when we deny the dreams, desires, and divine longings in our life. When we feel that we have been sent to do something, when we feel an urge to take a risk, to fulfill a bit of our destiny, but shrink back in fear, we whittle away parts of our soul.

Decker knew that the Creator wanted him to leave his hometown and work for a mission agency in Brazil serving some of the poorest people in the world. He had picked out the mission school that he felt he was being sent to. He had contacted the director of the school and had adequate savings to fund his schooling. He had the blessing of his family, and his spouse was going to follow him as soon as she could bring her job to an end. But he was frozen in place.

Decker was afraid of the risks he would have to take. It was going to be dangerous. He would be working with people who lived without clean water and medical supplies. Decker might indeed contract an illness that could kill him. What he failed to realize was that he could contract an illness that would kill him sitting on the couch in his own living room. Because Decker was paralyzed by this fear, each day, bit by bit, he died. He knew what he was supposed to do, he knew why he had been sent into the world, but he repeatedly and daily said no. It made him sick in his gut. Decker felt sullen and depressed because he couldn't bring himself to take the risk. Each day Decker said no, a bit of him died. He whittled away his soul.

Your Last Breath. The second death of your dying is the moment that your heart stops, your brain ceases all activity, your eyes glaze over, and your chest rattles like a gasp of breeze in a hollow cave. It's when the people around your bed look at each other and say, "Look, he just died."

You may have said that you don't want to be a burden for your loved ones after you die. Yet, if you have not prepared for your last breath, then you leave a pile of physical and emotional rocks that will weigh down your kin for years to come.

There are some obvious things that you need to do. Do you have a will? Have you worked through the issue of how to distribute your assets? If you have young children, have you decided who will raise them and how you want them raised? Have you designated someone for your power of attorney? Have you made it clear how long you want to be connected to life support systems, if at all? What do you want done with your body? Do you want to be cremated or do you want to be embalmed and buried? Have you picked out where you want your ashes scattered or your body buried? All of these are obvious questions that you can't shuffle aside.

A very helpful tool that I recommend is the workbook *Aging with Dignity: The Five Wishes.*[10] Jim Towey, an attorney who worked with Mother Theresa in Calcutta, founded the organization Aging with Dignity. Towey went on to do considerable work in death and dying. He found that people needed help in answering critical questions about the end of their lives.

- Whom do you want to make health care decisions for you when you can't make them?
- What kind of medical treatment do you want or not want?
- How comfortable do you want to be?
- How do you want people to treat you?
- What do you want your loved ones to know?

These questions can help guide you through these difficult issues. After you have done this work, make it abundantly clear to your friends and family what your "wishes" are for the end of your life.

More than the physical nature of this death, you need to come to terms with its spiritual aspects. What do you believe happens at the moment of your death? Do you believe that your body dies and you're just gone, or does something else happen? Do you believe that after you die you walk into paradise through the heavenly gates and enter the presence of the Creator? Or do you believe that your soul passes through a series of stages and then enters another being, reincarnated? Does your soul stay intact, or is it diffused throughout the cosmos? Bringing clarity to your beliefs about what happens after you die helps loosen the icy grip that the fear of dying can have on your life.

A very important part of the moment of your death is making sure that your loved ones know exactly how you feel about them.

Imagine that you are dying a slow death to cancer. You know it is coming. The doctors have said that there is nothing more they can do for you. It's now only a matter of months, weeks, or days before you die. Think about this: Whom do you want to come visit you? What do you want to say to them? Whom do you need to forgive? Of whom do you need to ask forgiveness? What do you need to say to your spouse, your business partner, your children, your neighbor, or your worst enemy? Now, what would it take to actually take the time to say these things while you and they are still living? Do it now, today. Be intentional. Choose it and do it.

My greatest teacher about death was Tom. The Creator sent Tom into my life when he was diagnosed with stage-four colon cancer. I worked with Tom as his spiritual mentor. However, he taught me more than I could ever offer him. Tom's death was a long, slow process in which the cancer carved him down. Tom lived on chemotherapy and pain medications for two years. In the months before he died, Tom said his last two years were the greatest gifts that had ever been given him. They allowed him to come to terms with all the questions about how he wanted to die. He made a will, designated a power of attorney, discerned how he felt about life support systems, and made it clear how he wanted his body dealt with after he died.

Those two years gave Tom the time to answer the question about what he believed would happen to him after he died. Tom and I had many long conversations about heaven, resurrection, and reincarnation. We talked about all the different spiritual traditions and what they taught about what happens to the soul. As we talked, he came to a state of personal clarity. He knew deep in his soul that when he died he was going to enter into the eternal presence of the Supreme Being.

One of the most beautiful things that Tom did in his last two years was to bring everybody he loved into his room. One by one he told them how much he loved and cared about them. These conversations helped remove Tom's fear about the moment of his death. When his days narrowed to a few, Tom had a sense of peace. His wife and his children surrounded him at the moment of his death. As I sat with Tom in his last hour, I could feel the room fill with a divine presence. His last hours were long and hard as his body fought to stay alive, but when his body relaxed and his soul was released, I knew exactly where Tom was—stepping into his greatest hopes and dreams.

What Is Your Legacy? The third death of your dying is the last moment your name is mentioned on the planet. Most of us never stop to think about this. When will be the last time your name is mentioned? Who will mention it? What will the context be? Will they be cursing your name or speaking of what a great blessing you were? It's a question of legacy.

All of us leave a legacy of some kind. When I work with a family planning a memorial service, I always ask, "What do you think is this person's legacy?" For some people, their legacy extends only to the generation in which they are living. They will die; people will come to their funeral. When it's over, the mourners will head to their cars and that will be it. The name of the deceased will never be mentioned again.

What a shame.

I once posed the legacy question to a family of adult children after their father died. They stared at me blankly. I started probing and eventually they answered, "Watching TV." It was all he did. He went to work, came home, and watched television until bed. He went to sleep with the television blaring. On weekends, all he did was watch television. He ate watching television. He even had a television in his bathroom. There were only his three adult children and a handful of people at this man's funeral. There was no reception afterward. We went to the cemetery, I said a few words, and he was lowered into the ground. He had a tiny headstone with his name and the date of his death. Period. His life was over. What did he leave behind? How long will his name be remembered? No more than the two minutes it took us to drive back through the gates of the cemetery.

It's amazing the impact that one person can have, and how that life can echo through the generations. Too often, though, that legacy comes from the darkness of wreaking havoc in people's lives.

Let's call her Becky. Unfortunately, this story describes thousands of people's lives. Becky came to talk to me about why she continued to marry alcoholics. She had been married and divorced three times, to alcoholics. Each time she divorced she swore she would never marry someone who drank and each time, she repeated the same story.

During our visit Becky and I drew on the whiteboard a genogram that depicted each generation of her family as far back as she knew. It started with her parents; each of them was an alcoholic. Then going back for generation upon generation there was at least one significant person who destroyed his or her life, and the family's life, with booze. It was a terrible legacy that Becky was perpetuating. We discussed the idea that part of the reason God sent Becky into the world was for her to break the pattern of alcoholism. We talked about seeking intense psychotherapy. Once she understood the impact that her forebears had on her life, she could start a new legacy of health and wholeness that could echo through future generations. To Becky's credit she sought that therapy and is now involved in a healthy relationship that is alcohol-free. It would be a glorious thing that after five generations her offspring could talk about their great-great-great-great-grandmother Rebecca, who had the courage to break the addictive cycle.

When will be the last time your name is mentioned on this planet? What kind of legacy will you leave? The question invites you to contemplate the way you are living right now. If you choose to embody the divine dream for your life, then you create a legacy that empowers others to do the same. Your adult children will want to talk to their children and friends about your largesse because of the way you touched them. They will hang your picture on the wall and every Thanksgiving they will talk about the blessing of your life. Either that or they will use it as a dartboard. Think about it; you are either a blessing or a curse. It's your choice.

Dealing with each one of these three deaths helps you overcome one of the greatest fears that people have—the fear of death. By taking actions and evaluating the different aspects of your life, you empower yourself to overcome your fear of death. Once you have been freed from your fear, you can take the risks to embody your purpose. But it's not the only fear that we have to overcome. Another fear that stymies people is the fear of not having enough money.

Money—The Golden Cuffs

It's a little "click" that we rarely hear. When the golden cuffs snap around our soul we are caught. At some place in our adult development, we settle for a certain income that provides a lifestyle that gives us comfort and security. When we attain that financial level the cuffs snap into place. We are locked into a particular life course. We have to earn this amount of money to provide for this lifestyle. Now this may be a great joy if what you are doing is what the Creator sent you to do. Then the golden cuffs will not be cuffs at all, but golden wings that empower you in your divine destiny. The challenge becomes when what you have grown accustomed to is not what you were sent to do. All along, you hold the key. Only you can unlock the golden cuffs.

Some people are never able to slip free. They choose security over adventure. Unfortunately these people also daily die the first death. Choosing security exacts a hefty price. You may be financially secure, but your soul will feel as if it has been sold out.

There is no getting around it: fulfilling your divine destiny may be a huge financial sacrifice. You may have to sell your home to afford to go back to school. You may have to sell your vehicles. You may have to cash in retirement savings. You may have to move across the country or to the other side of the globe. You have been sent. It is going to cost you something. It's the price you are asked to pay.

There is also a great upside to fulfilling the Creator's dream for you. When you are keyed into your passion, when you are pursuing your joy, often you find that money isn't really a concern, because your life is full and satisfied. You find the income that you earn is enough to meet all of your life requirements. Marsha Sinetar's book *Do What You Love and the Money Will Follow*[11] makes it abundantly clear. When you are following your passion, money flows to you. The Ultimate Being does not intend for you to be destitute. You may not be among the wealthiest people in the world, but you will be rich beyond comparison. When my children were little they used to wish we were "super rich!" I would tell them, "We are! We're the wealthiest people I know!" "How?" they would whine. "Look at the stupid car we drive." I would respond, "We have each other, we have a home, we have macaroni and cheese for dinner tonight—your favorite! We have books to read, you have a great school, and you have parents who love you! You're rich!" I'm convinced that this is when they first learned the most significant skill of any child—the eye-roll of disgust.

Some people are sent into the world to make money. It sounds strange but it is true. Ben had the Midas touch. From a very early age he knew that he was going to be wealthy. From his childhood lawn business to the international corporation he founded and now leads, Ben always had huge amounts of cash. His work is his divine destiny. Ben is also a very faithful man. His wealth brings incredible responsibility. He annually donates millions to charitable causes. Each day Ben makes sure he has used his wealth to further the Creator's purposes in the world. Many people would love to have that responsibility. I think we need to be cautious to wish for that burden. As Jesus said, "It is easier for a camel to go through the eye of a needle than for someone who is rich to enter the kingdom of God."[12] The wealthy have the responsibility to make sure that their money is a reflection of the economic justice the Creator desires.

I believe that there are many people like Ben sent into the world. They are like the characters from Jesus's parable of the talents—the first had three talents, while another had two, and the third, one. The individual with the three talents had the greater responsibility to use the wealth for the Master's benefit.

Financially wealthy people will also tell you about the snap of the financial cuffs. When wealthy folks feel that their divine purpose is counter to the one that they are currently living, they often have to take a huge gulp as they struggle to slip free of the golden cuffs around their soul.

In the Christian New Testament, the author of 1 Timothy says, "The love of money is a root of all kinds of evil."[13] Note that it's not money that's the root of all evil, but people's feelings toward it. I could just as easily say, "Anxiety about money is the root of all evil," or "The fear of not having enough money is the root of all evil." If fears about money are a stumbling block to fulfilling the divine dream for your life, then your soul is cuffed.

Where the Creator provides the vision, it will also provide the means. When you step out in faith to courageously fulfill your destiny, financial doors seem to slide open. Too often people get caught up in the "how." How can I afford this change in my life? How can I afford to put a roof over my head? How can I afford the education that I need? All of these are reasonable questions, but ultimately they get in the way of fulfilling the Creator's sacred dream.

Sometimes you are not supposed to know how; you are just supposed to do and trust that the "how" will emerge. When you start engaging your purpose, the way to proceed appears. People rise up to guide you, ideas develop that lead you, and opportunities develop to support you. These are not coincidences. It is how the Ultimate Being colludes with your action. It's why Jesus taught so clearly about worry, fear, and money. To fulfill the divine dream for your life, you have to let go of your fear of money and trust that your needs will be provided for.

Looking Like a Fool

The lights were set just right. I had dressed in an angel costume made especially for me. I had huge wings that spread behind me and I had written and rehearsed a special message to preach on Christmas Eve. The plan was to have ethereal music playing as I walked out in front of the congregation as the Angel Gabriel. I asked my staff countless times, "Are you sure this is a good idea? Isn't this stretching things a bit? Aren't we going over the top here?" They assured me over and over, "No, this is fine, it'll work, don't worry." When it came time, the lights dimmed, the music came up, the rear lights came on, and I walked out—the Angel Gabriel appeared.

People were aghast and laughing. The back lights were so bright they shone through the angel outfit. All I had on underneath was a pair of running tights. I looked buck naked under the gown.

After the service some people were polite. They shook my hand and left. Others were blunt and straight to the point, "You ruined my Christmas Eve." "Where did you ever get such a stupid idea?" "That was hilarious! You were the naked angel!"

. . . I felt like a fool.

I wish I could say that was the only time I felt like a fool. There was the time I told a congregation after singing a hymn to "Shit down." I can tell you about countless times when people got up and walked out of sermons. I have realized over the years that I am a cure for insomnia—people fall asleep just listening to me preach. I don't mean to, but sometimes in the heat of the moment I say stupid things. I forget people's names; I announce things that were supposed to be a surprise. Over the years I have tried to rein in my tongue, but some evenings I sit on the edge of my bed and say to myself, "Man, you really looked like a fool today."

There is only one way I have gotten over it and that has been to remind myself that this is why I was sent into the world. I know in the depths of my soul that I have been sent to wake people up to the Creator's presence through speaking, teaching, and writing. Knowing this helps me get back on my feet each time I fail. I have spoken professionally over 3,500 times, and each time I step before a group of people I have to overcome the fear of looking like a fool.

It comes with the turf. To fulfill your destiny requires risk, thinking outside the box, and sometimes looking like a fool. In the Christian New Testament, the apostle Paul said that we are fools for Christ.[14] That is so true. People will tell you that you are being foolish. When you choose to change careers, to sacrifice security, to speak out on controversial issues, when you reach out in compassion or go against the wishes of your family and friends, people will call you foolish.

The fear of looking like a fool keeps people from responding to the destiny of their lives. They are afraid that people might belittle, mock, and reject them. They are so afraid that they don't take risks, and they choose not to fulfill their destiny.

Here's the kicker. They *will* . . .

belittle, mock, and reject you. If you are going to fulfill the Creator's destiny for your life, you have to get used to it. Take comfort that when this happens it puts you in pretty good company. As Jesus said, "For in the same way they persecuted the prophets who were before you."[15]

When the Baha'u'llah, the spiritual leader of the Baha'i religion, shared that God had sent him as the next unique divine manifestation to fulfill the teachings of Jesus and Mohammed, he was jailed and tortured. His family and friends were ostracized. His followers were arrested and beaten.

Many people do not associate persecution with the Buddha. They forget that King Ajatashatru and Devadatta, the Buddha's cousin, sought to kill him when he taught the Lotus Sutra. They unleashed a wild elephant to stampede him. They kidnapped and killed his followers. They tried to kill the Buddha by dropping rocks on him as he walked down the road. Other stories relate that women were bribed into filing false charges of sexual impropriety.[16]

If you are going to pursue your destiny, you have to be willing to have egg on your face. When you take risks, inevitably you will be wrong. You will stick your neck out and say something emphatically, only to be proven inaccurate. People will use this to discredit your reputation, your integrity, and that which you are striving to pursue. They will stand before you and throw emotional eggs that feel like spit in your face.

It takes the hide of a rhino to endure the egg and spit. Rhino Liner is a sticky tar-like substance you can spray on the bed of a pickup truck. It protects the metal bed from the debris that is thrown into the back of a truck. To embody your divine purpose you need this same kind of liner, a thick skin that shields you from the onslaught of negativity that may be poured out on you. When you have just received an unusual amount of criticism, you will need to take your hand and rub it over the top of your arm and remind yourself, "Thick skin, baby, you need to have thick skin."

It also takes the sensitivity of a stethoscope. The Ultimate Being sends people to heal the world and minister to the pain of people's lives. If all you have is thick skin, you miss the heartbeat of pain. Do you remember the first time your childhood doctor held the stethoscope up to your chest so that you could hear your own heart beating? Do you remember being stunned at the lub-dub of your own lifeblood? While you need thick skin to deal with the eggs thrown your way, you also need a gentle sensitivity to hear the longings and desires of people's souls.

Standing Alone

Andy was waiting for me in the dark hallway after a meeting. As I opened the door I saw that his eyes had been rubbed red with hours of crying. His wife had died months before. Since her death Andy had lost all traction in his life. For years Andy's sole purpose had been to take care of his wife. He had abandoned or alienated all friends and other family members. Since she died he had felt completely and totally alone. There was no one to turn to for love and support. He was facing what most of us fear, the isolated feeling of being alone in the midst of a vast globe of people.

As humans, we have a deep need to be together embedded in us. It's a survival instinct. We are designed to be in community. The fear of being alone is grounded deep within the fear of dying as a solitary, forgotten person.

We think that if we are alone we are not okay, we are not acceptable. When we find ourselves in a solitary situation we wonder what has caused other people to reject us. When we are alone it is hard not to think, "What is so wrong with me, that people don't want to be with me?" Yet this is the situation in which countless numbers of people find themselves. They are alone. They are single without a life partner. They are middle-aged and their loved one has died. They are unemployed and have no colleagues. They live in a suburb that is teeming with people, yet they don't know anyone.

My ministry is in the midst of a sprawling suburb, yet one of the most common complaints that bring people to my office is that they are feeling lonely. Here they are, surrounded by rows of houses, some of them not more than ten feet apart, and yet they feel alone. They don't know their neighbors, they are cut off from family, and they have no one to talk to.

The only way to overcome the fear of being alone begins with being comfortable in your own skin. People who know who they are, who know their identity, their values, and purpose find they are just as comfortable being alone as they are with other people. When you completely accept yourself as a person of worth and value, then being with other people is a grace, not a necessity.

You need to become comfortable with being alone if you are going to fulfill your destiny. While later I present the need to work and collaborate with others, an important truth is that you may find yourself standing alone. The crowd may be going in one direction and yet you will know that you have been sent to go another way. It's like the prophets from the Jewish faith; their message was so unpopular that kings threatened them, people ran from them, and they were shut out of their synagogues. Yet HaShem sent them to speak about justice to the kings, to the empire, and to the people. They had to overcome their fear of being alone to fulfill their divine destiny.

One of the saddest stories from the life of Jesus comes when he was preaching a sermon and one-by-one people got up and left him until he was standing alone. The truth that he was teaching was so offensive they just could not stand to hear what he had to say.[17] Yet Jesus did not allow his fear of being alone to deter him from proclaiming his message. Instead, he was so grounded in what he had to say that it gave him strength to continue on despite the solitary nature of his purpose.

When you are grounded in the truth that you know about yourself, in your sense of identity, then you stand alone in a way that strengthens you. I think this was the reason Jesus sought times to be alone. Because of the challenge before him, he constantly needed to return to the presence of the Creator. What gave him the strength to speak his truth was the knowledge that he was fulfilling a divine mandate. He knew that he had been sent and that was all he needed.

The same is true for you. As you continue down the path toward fulfilling your purpose, you will need to be reminded of the reason you are doing what you're doing. Other people's approval is not enough to keep you going, especially when they withhold that approval. The strength to continue on comes from knowing that this is not a willy-nilly dream that you're pursuing. No, you are doing this because you have been sent.

While people may abandon and walk away from you, the Creator never does. Knowing this empowers you to let go of the anxiety of needing other people's approval. As Krishna said to Arjuna in the Bhagavad Gita, "The Lord dwells deep in the heart of all beings. . . . Arjuna, take refuge in him alone; by his kindness you will attain the state of imperishable peace."[18] What more do you need? The Creator is with you.

When you stand at a spiritual crossroads and you are struggling to discern what God has sent you to do, you must come to terms with your fears. Are you afraid of death and dying? Does the fear of the lack of money make you hesitate? Looking like a fool is never easy, but does it make you stop dead in your tracks? Does your fear of being alone compromise what you are to do? Let's be honest, these fears are valid and real. Yet, when you understand your fears and how they hold you back, that understanding helps you identify what your fears are keeping you from. Your fears are a central insight leading you to the divine convergence.

What Is Your Anger?

The divine convergence is beginning. You are in touch with your passions. You celebrate your joys. You admit to your fears. The next question you need to ask is, "What's my anger?"

What do you take umbrage with? What riles you and makes you mad? What do you feel is unjust? The Creator who sent you into the world has a bias for justice. The Hebrew Prophets of the Jewish faith were sent into the world to address the poverty and injustice of the nations of Judah and Israel. In some way, each of us has been sent into the world to address the injustices that afflict humanity. Whether poverty, hunger, unemployment, or ideologies that limit free thought, anything that keeps people from enjoying the abundance of the creation angers the Supreme Being. To discern your destiny you have to get in touch with what angers you. Your anger is one of the keys revealing your purpose.

When people think of Jesus they think of someone who was meek and mild. While he was someone who welcomed children onto his lap, he was never afraid to confront the injustice of his day. In one particular story Jesus had a violent outburst that would land us in jail if we tried to do the same. Jesus sat outside the temple watching the moneychangers swindle the pilgrims that came for the Passover sacrifice.

Peasants came from the countryside to sacrifice their unblemished lambs to have their sins forgiven. They had to wait in long lines often to find that their lambs, after inspection, were not suitable and were often confiscated. They could either buy a temple lamb at an exorbitant price or be forced to buy a lesser animal to sacrifice, a dove. But unfortunately they didn't have the right type of temple coins as they came from the countryside, where there was a different currency. Before they bought a dove they had to have their money exchanged. In the exchange they were charged a hefty tax. The peasants who wanted to come to the temple to have their sins forgiven were instead swindled. Jesus sat on the edge of the crowd watching the whole proceedings and became outraged. He stormed through the crowds, flipped over tables, and drove out the moneychangers.[19] Now while I don't encourage the actual flipping of tables, as this often leads to anger management classes, the story shows Jesus's frustration. He was angry with anybody who placed impediments between the people and God. It raised his lip in a bit of a spiritual snarl.

How does it feel to see Jesus angry? It should empower you. It should help you not be afraid of your own anger or discontent. Maybe by looking at Jesus you will see that your anger is a divine gift awakening you to the reason you are on this planet. Your anger could just be the fuel that motivates you to fulfill your destiny.

Are you angry about the way senior citizens are being treated in the nursing home near you? Does the stunning depth of poverty in your community grip your gut? Does it blow your mind that the huge demand for illegal drugs in the United States creates dangerous and lethal drug cartels in Mexico and Central America? If so, then I applaud your discontent. It means you are hot on the trail of your divine purpose.

The Creator did not send you into the world just for your own benefit. Ultimately, it's not all about you. You will find meaning not only when you fulfill your destiny, but also when you use this purpose to relieve the pain and burdens of others. This is how divine justice works. The scales of abundance are unbalanced in the world. While it was intended that all partake equally in the riches of the planet, the world is far from perfect. Evil people and oppressive systems blanket people's lives like thick smog. The Supreme Being intervenes and addresses these inequalities by filling people with passions and a sense of righteous indignation. When you give yourself permission to be honest and vocal about what angers you, you tap into the depth of meaning that drives your purpose. Your anger is a guide and a thread that leads you to divine insights. So go ahead, make a list. Get honest. What makes you angry? Spill it out and get real with it, feel the burn in your heart, and you will feel a holy fire burning in your soul.

What Are Your Gifts?

If you are engaging this process of discernment, sitting before you are your passions, your joys, and your fears; now I want you to identify your gifts.

It's time for another list. List your ten unique gifts—things that you do well, really well. There is only one you. You have particular gifts, and the way you express these gifts in the world is unique. I suggest you number a clean piece of paper from one to ten and make your list now. . . .

Don't be shy. Don't hide your light under a bushel. Is it cooking, changing oil in cars, nursing, planning a city's waste system? Get it out. I'm serious. This is no time for humility. This is just between you and the Creator. Be proud. You have been given these gifts, so get crystal clear with what was planted deep in your soul. You should be able to rattle off these top ten things as easily as you can recite the ABCs.

If you are going to suck up the courage to live your divine destiny you are going to need a little swagger about your gifts. You are going to need some courage and confidence. The Jewish scriptures tell the story of King David, when as a small boy he confronted the Philistine giant Goliath. David trusted a small pile of stones and a slingshot. Your gifts are your pile of stones. The challenges in your life are your Goliath. To succeed you need to launch your gifts against the looming giants that challenge you.

The fact that you know you are really good at something doesn't mean that you are prideful, arrogant, or rude about your abilities. Your confidence should create the exact opposite emotion—humility. Your sense of inner confidence should open you to experience the ways other people use and express these same gifts.

While your gifts were freely given, it takes a lifetime of effort on your part to hone them into perfection. The greatest advice I ever received was to constantly work to perfect my gifts and never to take them for granted.

Malcolm Gladwell, in his book *Outliers: The Story of Success*, writes about the ten-thousand-hour rule.[20] To develop a basic competency in any one area, a person needs to invest at least ten thousand hours of work. This concept is the bedrock of self-development. Everybody you think is naturally gifted will tell you that, while the gift may be natural, perfecting it has taken a lifetime. The best athletes are the first on the practice field and the last to leave. The same with musicians, writers, speakers, engineers, wood workers; literally anybody with a talent (that would be you) who takes him- or herself seriously is constantly working to improve. You have to develop the discipline to carve out time to hone your craft. The fact that you have been sent doesn't mean you will arrive ready to rock and roll. To develop your gifts you will need to find a mentor to guide you, a place for education, a community of like-minded people to learn with, and an audience to practice in front of. Where there is practice there is failure. In the midst of the ten thousand hours you will make at least twenty thousand mistakes. It comes with the territory. Get used to it. That's why you have to have a rhino hide, be willing to have egg on your face, and not fear standing alone in a crowd. Also, remember that the ten thousand hours is just to achieve basic competency. To truly excel could easily take another ten thousand hours. This is why anybody with a sharply honed gift is a person of great humility. The more you grow, the more you realize what you don't know. Instead of demoralizing you, this knowledge fuels a desire to grow and mature to new heights.

One of the hardest and yet most important aspects of developing your gifts is having a good editor. William Stafford was one of the great poets of American literature. His poetry is elegant and brilliant. I had the opportunity to hear Mr. Stafford speak on several occasions. One of the lessons he taught was that editors are our friends. He never shied away from their insights and openly allowed them to critique his work. I take his teaching to heart. Before this book found its way into your hands several people critiqued and guided my writing. The editors at Quest showed me a path of writing that took this book to heights that I would never have seen on my own. You too, need an editor. You need people who will give you honest feedback about how you are using your gifts. Even those people who are harshly critical of you, those who walk out on you or belittle you, can be a wonderful source of insight. These negative people can be your greatest guides. Their negativity can help you learn not to take things personally and to stay committed to your direction. They can teach you how to rise above and go beyond your feelings. They will teach you the fine art of wiping off yolks and toughening the hide. Editors and critics are the ones who ultimately strengthen you on your path.

The Creator's dreams are going to unfold around your gifts. You were not sent to fulfill destinies that you weren't prepared for. Your gifts were intentionally planted within your luminescence before you were conceived. When you know and claim your gifts and invest the ten thousand hours, you have the right tools to begin to discern your divine destiny.

You will know your gifts because for you, developing and using these skills is like going down a slide. They are as natural to you as using your hands. They are so natural that you will often take them for granted. While others stand back in awe at how you handle children, thread a needle, raise a garden, you will comment, "This? . . . Why, it was nothing!" It was nothing because it was a gift that was bestowed on you.

I just had carpeting put in my home. Jack, the installer, was one of the most talented men I had ever seen. He would measure a room and stand and stare. He would mutter to himself, then jot a few notes. Then he would be off to the next room. He would go back out to the roll of carpet stretched out on the driveway and pause like a man in prayer. He cut the carpet like a surgeon slicing into a brain. I was mesmerized by the way he laid out the carpet and seamed it together. For two days I stood in his way as he cut, seamed, and stretched the carpet in place. He was filled with joy the entire time he was working. Carpet was his passion. He would talk my ear off about brands, styles, and ways of cutting. When I asked him how he found his way into the carpet business he said, "I was *sent* here to install carpets!" My jaw dropped! I then described to him this book and he just chuckled, "Yup, that's me! I was sent to install carpets." He had the natural gifts to lay carpet: the strength of a bull, the mind of a mathematician, and an artist's flair for beauty. He had also invested thousands of hours over thirty years. He had spent more time on his knees than a monk in a monastery. The outcome was a man who knew the joy of packing up his tools at the end of the day, having fulfilled the reason the Creator had sent him here.

And you? What is it that you have been graced with? In the moment that the Supreme Being held the luminescence of your soul, an abundance of gifts were planted within you. If you are going to discern your divine destiny you need to be keenly aware of your natural abilities and have the discipline to develop them.

The Convergence

The way your holy destiny emerges around the convergence of your answers to these questions is magical. When you hold your passions, joys, fears, anger, and gifts in front of you, bathe them in prayer and contemplation; the Creator's dreams materialize before your eyes. The convergence is the power of the Tao embodied as te. Your actions are effortless; you find a groove where time disappears; you are wu-wei. These three Taoist concepts are tools to help us understand the dynamic that occurs in the divine convergence.

The Tao is the power of the Cosmic Being. Like a giant prism it magnifies Brahman, HaShem, God, and Allah. The Tao, like these other deities, is a force that moves through the cosmos. It is the flow of the Ganges River, it is the power of Ganesh, and it is the movement of the Holy Spirit. When an individual opens up to the flow of the Tao, taking intentional steps to move as the Tao moves, the power realized is te. When the divine convergence collides in a human soul the power of te is unstoppable. A person attains great insight and has amazing endurance. The actions of a person who is living his or her te are effortless; this is wu-wei.

Wu-wei is described as action/nonaction. Wu-wei was Michael Jordan on a basketball court; it was Mozart writing an opera; it is you when you do something that is so natural that you move just like grease on a griddle. You have stepped into wu-wei when work flows from your hands without thinking. It is after ten thousand hours of practice that words glide from your fingers, stitches fly across fabric, or CAD drawings emerge as if by magic.

The meshing of the divine convergence is Tao, te, and wu-wei. Like a tulip that can't help but break through soil and burst into magnificent color, you will do the same. As a giant sequoia grows to a great height because it is doing exactly what it was meant to do, so will you. When the convergence of the five questions explodes in your consciousness, the power of the Tao moves through you. Te will be the strength of your character. Your actions will be effortless; you will embody wu-wei.

Let's say your passion is cooking. You love to cook lamb rubbed with sage and rosemary. Red peppers explode with aroma when you stir-fry them with carrots, sea salt, and asparagus. In front of the stove you are in your element. This is wu-wei.

You don't just watch the cooking shows—you ingest them. You constantly read cookbooks, you love shopping for cookware, you have a knack for exploring new recipes, and you have an innate sense of the ways that spices accentuate certain meats. For some reason your insight sparks when you open a cupboard. This is te. It is your power.

Your joy is setting the table for a particular event. There is no such thing as casual dining for you. Even the most ordinary meal is an extraordinary event. Your real joy comes when you see the smiles on people's faces as they relish each bite of what you have prepared for them. You know that you blossom as an individual when you cook. You feel that it is not just something you enjoy, but something you were meant to do. You feel silly when you say this, but when you are cooking you feel a cosmic connection to all people through the ages who have prepared food. You know the depth of the responsibility to feed people and the joy of seeing people dive into a meal. This is Tao moving through you. You are the tulip and the sequoia, because you are doing what you "naturally do."

As much as you enjoy cooking, though, you secretly harbor the fear of making people sick and then looking like a fool. You're afraid the cleanliness police are going to show up someday in your kitchen and prevent you from ever cooking again.

Your anger is stirred by the amount of hunger you see in the world. Every time you turn on the news, the stories that grip you the most are stories of famine. You can't stand seeing pictures of people lined up for food. When you drive down the road and see men and women holding up signs that say, "Will work for food," you have the desire to take them home to feed them. When your temple has a food drive you clean out your pantries and donate everything you have.

Your gifts are clear. You know you can cook. You are very creative and you know how to plan and organize. You have a keen business sense and know budgeting and accounting. You are a people person with the gift of making folks feel at home and welcomed.

You have felt for some time that your job as a school principal is not what you are supposed to be doing. Is it meaningful? Yes. Does it pay well? Yes. Are you making a difference in people's lives? Of course. But, lately, the feeling that you are supposed to be doing something different doesn't go away. When you hear a homily on using your gifts, you cringe inside because, while you are very successful, you know that what you are doing is not the purpose for which you have been sent into the world.

After praying and meditating on the issue, after talking with your spouse and friends, you decide to make a major career change. You announce that at the end of the semester you are going to resign and open a restaurant. But it won't just be any restaurant; a portion of your food will be donated to the local homeless shelters. You want your restaurant to be a driving force to end hunger in your city.

People think you're nuts. At night when you are trying to fall asleep, *you* think you're nuts. Your fear of making people ill through your cooking grabs you. Your fear of being inspected by the health department is now a reality. You struggle with the fear of having enough money. Why give up a great job and a secure pension? What if no one comes to the restaurant and you have to close it down? Not only will you be bankrupt—you'll look like a fool. The fears almost stifle you. What keeps you going, though, is that the people who know you best think that you have finally come to your senses and you will be pursuing your passion.

While it is a struggle to open the restaurant, the vision carries you through the financing, the purchasing of the building, the remodeling of the space, and hiring employees. You are amazed how time after time just the right person emerges with the perfect piece of information you need to take the next step. At times it feels as if there is an invisible force moving through you and for you. After the first year of running the restaurant and feeding not only the people who come in your doors, but also the homeless on the city streets, you feel as though you have found yourself. Every single one of your gifts is being utilized to its full potential. You have a smile that extends down to your soul because you know that you are living your divine destiny. Tulip . . . , Sequoia . . . , they are you.

Here's another scenario.

You have just been told that you have stage-four lung cancer. With treatment you may have a few years, at best, to live. Suddenly the question, what is the meaning of life, especially the meaning of *your life*, comes into sharp focus. With whatever time you have left, you want every minute to count. Since your days are numbered, there is almost a panic that sets in: you don't want to waste another twenty-four hours. At the church you attend you heard your pastor foolishly share the idea that God has sent you into the world for a reason. You begin to wonder, "Is having cancer really a part of the reason I was sent? If so, it is rather cruel." You set aside your feelings of frustration for a moment and grab a journal. On each separate page you write the questions that your pastor mentioned: passions, joys, fears, anger, and gifts.

What's your passion? Without a doubt, it's fishing. Your whole life you've loved to fish. As a kid you walked along the creeks and rivers by your house and fished for carp and bluegill. As an adult you love to fish—any kind of fishing. You love to watch fishing shows on Saturday morning and pore over catalogs of fishing equipment. Your garage is full of fishing poles, line, lures, waders, and boats. Your friends laugh that you really are a redneck because your basement wall is lined with mounted trout, salmon, bass, and steelhead that you've caught.

Your joy is very simple. You love being on the water. Your soul opens up as a fly line uncurls over a stream. When you are out on the ocean and a huge salmon breaks the water and dances across the surface, you can feel your own soul leap for joy. What you love even more is sharing these times with friends, especially children. You feel vitally alive when you take your kids out on the water and teach them to fish. It brings you such joy to hear them shout out, "I've got one! I've got one!" and see them reel in a beautiful fish.

Your fear stares you down like a big dog. You fear dying—plain and simple. It's not an imaginary tale that will happen someday. It's now. Your number has come up. Tears drop down and stain the page as you write, "I'm terrified of being dead."

But as you explore the thought even more, you realize that it's not just dying, it's being forgotten that grabs your soul. Will your children forget you? Will your grandchildren forget you? You begin thinking about the legacy that you are going to leave behind.

The next page: "What's my anger?" "That's simple," you think. "I'm angry that I have to die!" As you continue writing you realize that what really bugs you is how the rivers in your state are being overfished. It seems as though people don't give a damn about the purity of the river or the health of the fishery for the generations yet to come.

You turn the page: "What are my gifts?" It doesn't seem like much—you are an accountant, a bean counter. You sit behind a desk and add columns. Admittedly, you're good at it, very good. You also know that you are a devoted father and husband. Your gift is working behind the scenes. You don't like to be in the limelight; you like to work behind the curtain making sure the entire effort is successful.

You stare at this journal for what seems like hours. You're not much of a writer; this seems like a waste of time and energy. Here you are going to die, and yet you wonder if there ever was a purpose for your life.

The next day you are reading in the sports page about a group in your state called Trout Unlimited.[21] You have heard their name before but you were too busy with work to get involved with their projects. But now time is of the essence. You decide you are going to attend their next meeting. When you get to the meeting and step through the door it feels as if you have walked into a little piece of heaven. Here is a group talking about things you love and worry about—fish, fishing, and the health of rivers and streams. That night they announce that they need a treasurer for the group. Although you are new, you volunteer and they accept. You are welcomed by a group of strangers into a like-minded community. The entire evening you have an eerie sense that spiritual doors are opening for you, that a divine hand is guiding you.

Over the next months you become more involved in their work, you attend fund-raisers, and you go on group fishing outings. You take your kids on fishing trips with the group. You make friendships that would last a lifetime—in your case, a year, maybe two, even three. Over that span of time you talk with your new friends about your illness and they rally behind you. The entire time you wonder why it took getting cancer for you to find your spiritual home. Through the organization you feel as if you have found your place in the world, your life purpose, your spiritual destiny, the reason you were sent into the world.

This is how it happens when you meditate on the five questions; they converge into profound insights that lead you in life. Let me share just one more scenario.

You feel blessed beyond measure. You love your work, your home, your vehicles and the material possessions that you own. You don't feel that you live extravagantly by any means, but you just love where you are in life. As you are commuting to work one day, as the sun is coming up, you feel completely and totally at peace. While you drive you are praying with your eyes open and giving thanks to the Creator, when a blue Honda Accord crashes into you, sending you sailing into oncoming traffic, where you smash head-on into a grey Suburban. You don't remember much, only the numbness, the sirens, broken glass, and the firefighters. They pull you from the wreckage and then things begin to blur.

You are told you have been in a coma for days. You awake to IV bags, casts, and some very bad news. Your spinal cord has been severed. You are paralyzed from the waist down.

You lie in your hospital bed in shock; how can this be! My life was perfect just the way it was. You shriek in your mind, and then you shriek out loud, "How could God do this to me!"

The next months are filled with the struggle of rehabilitation, learning how to use a wheelchair, learning to navigate through the basics of life. Suddenly, nothing is easy, from going to the bathroom, to dressing yourself, to cooking.

During rehab your emotions are a roller coaster. You feel depressed, angry, bitter, and lonely. You crash into your fears like a freight train. "Will I be like this for the rest of my life? How will I make a living? Can I keep my job? Will my friends accept me and love me? How will I drive? How will I navigate around my apartment?" The fears hound you as each day presents more challenges.

One day your rabbi comes to visit you in the rehab center. His visit provides the perfect opportunity for you to ask the question that has been on the forefront of your mind: "How can HaShem do this to me? My life was so perfect; it was going so well. Am I being punished?" You long to have answers to these spiritual questions that have been nagging at your soul like a dark cloud.

Slowly, calmly, your rabbi explains to you that you are not being punished, but accidents happen to us. Tragedies come screaming out of nowhere and seemingly wreck our lives. We have blue Honda

Accords, cancer, strokes, earthquakes, and fires. These events completely alter our existence. It's not that HaShem does these things to us; it's more that they are a part of life.

Your rabbi provides an important insight that you ponder. Your car wreck was not a part of a divine plan for your life. Tragedy is not a part of HaShem's intentions. Your rabbi looks deep into your eyes and says words that ring in your heart, "What you need to know is that your life is not finished. HaShem isn't finished with you and does not abandon you. Instead, HaShem has been working from the moment of your accident to surround you with people who will help you rebuild your life. It's going to take time, maybe a lot of time. But you and HaShem will rebuild your life and you will find a new sense of purpose, a new sense of meaning and direction."

Those words buoy you. It's true; from the firefighters on the scene of the wreck, to the doctors and nurses at the rehab hospital, people have encouraged you every step of the journey. You had a conversation with one of your rehab nurses about why they spend their lives working with people who have had their lives wrecked by accidents. You were shocked and humbled when he explained that it was his divine purpose, his destiny. He feels as though he has been given special gifts and abilities to do this work. It's more than a job to him; it's why he was sent into the world.

"*Why he was sent into the world . . .* " You ponder this thought over and over. While you are learning to move your wheelchair over curbs, in and out of cars, and through narrow grocery aisles, you're thinking, "Does HaShem really send people into the world? Have I been sent here for something?"

As you scream at the frustration of kitchen counters too high, bathroom faucets out of reach, and heavy glass doors that refuse to stay open as they crash against your chair, you find yourself thinking, "What have I been sent to do?"

For months you think to yourself, "There's no way that I've been sent to do anything. Maybe there was a purpose before this stupid accident, but not now. No way!"

You return to work. They receive you with open arms and they have made many accommodations for your chair. It's good to be back with your coworkers and you almost forget about the chair and the term "disabled." You feel empowered to continue with your life.

As the weeks and months roll by and you adjust more to your new condition, you find yourself thinking back to what your rabbi said: "HaShem isn't finished with you." You begin to think about HaShem's presence in your life since the wreck. Instead of HaShem's feeling absent, looking back you can see how a divine presence was with you through the nurses, doctors, and therapists that worked with you all these many months. You feel something needling you, nudging, pushing, longing for something more, something deeper in your life.

One evening a therapist from the rehab center calls and invites you to come back to the center. Every year they have a reunion of folks who have successfully moved through the process and reentered their lives. At the reunion, graduates are invited to speak and interact with folks who are in the midst of their rehabilitation.

At first you are hesitant. Do you want to go back there? The thought of it brings a sense of nausea as you relive the trauma and the difficulty of rehab. In a flash you remember the tears, pain, and depression of putting your life back together. But something nudges and pushes you to go back. So you do.

As you roll through the front doors of the center you are greeted by laughter, hugs, and handshakes. It's inspiring to see how the other people are doing, those whose lives were wrecked by accidents, strokes, and injuries. You feel an amazing bond with these people; you have all faced down death. You have had to overcome all of your fears and dig down deep to rebuild your lives. You realize that you are not just survivors; you really have thrived.

That afternoon, it all comes back to you like waves on the beach, insight after insight, memory after memory. When you roll by the therapy pool you bring your chair to a sudden stop. In the pool a therapist holds a young teenager who is flailing in the water. An accident has come crashing into his life and his youthful passion has been reduced to this—thrashing with terror in a pool. His eyes fill with tears as the therapist calms him and helps him relax in the water. As you sit there watching, you remember so vividly your first time in the pool and the fear you had of drowning. It's all so clear, so vivid. You want to reach out and tell him, "You're going to be all right. Just relax. I was right where you are and look where I am today." It's then that you hear it, crystal clear, "So tell him." You look behind you to see who said it. Nobody is there. You hear it again, but this time it's an urgent nudging deep in your soul, "So tell him! Do it. Now!"

You roll right up to the edge of the pool. Your voice hesitates, catches, you choke a tear. Then you say it, "You're going to be all right. You need to relax. Trust your therapist. You'll get over the fear of drowning. I did, less than a year ago. If I can do it, so can you." In that moment a door in your soul opens.

As you visit each room of the rehab center you find yourself chatting with all the clients. You speak words of encouragement. You urge people to not give up, but to keep on working, sweating, trying something one more time. With each new conversation a place in your soul opens wider and wider. You find yourself smiling and laughing. The words of hope that you have been giving to others have actually been lifting you.

That first visit was the beginning of what would become a whole new phase of your life. In addition to your job, you now volunteer countless hours at the rehab center. You lead support groups. Your people skills are being used to their full potential. You speak regularly to victims and families, and your presence brings hope to those in the midst of putting their lives back together. While you have a job where you make a living, at the rehab center you have found your life. Every time you roll through the front doors you feel as if you have stepped into your true self. There is a sense of oneness that you have at the center. You are one with the clients and therapists, but even more, you are one with HaShem. You realize that your rabbi was indeed right; HaShem was not finished with you. There was a whole new phase of your life that was waiting to blossom and grow. You were indeed sent to fulfill a purpose.

The scenarios of people discovering their holy destiny are as myriad as the number of people on the planet. Every story is unique, as each person is a unique child of the Creator. The process that you engage in to discern your divine destiny will not be as smooth as the scenarios I presented. Life is much more complicated. You will have moments of clarity and times of deep spiritual fog. But if you want to know why you are here, I encourage you to ask these questions: "What are my passions? What is my joy? What are my fears? What is my anger? What are my gifts?" Keep asking them until you start seeing connections between them and how you fill your days. Is your life filled with passion? Do you delight in being alive? Does joy spread through you? Are you being challenged to overcome your fears? Are you using your gifts to respond to the frustrations and challenges that people have to live with? When you spend time working through these questions, a convergence happens; things come together. Everyone realizes it in a different way. For some people their divine destiny strikes like lightning. Other people experience their purpose as an insight that wells from within them like a whale breaching on the surface of the ocean. Many people experience it like a pear ripening on a tree. The divine convergence happens repeatedly in each stage of life. Again, you don't have one destiny, but you have many. Like a stream flowing down a mountain, your life twists and turns. At each moment there is something pulsing within you, a force urging you on.

You have this one life—one life. You are here for a reason. You can discern why the Creator sent you here. It's not a mystery; it's a convergence between a divine dream and your willingness to intentionally embody it.

Questions to Help You Discover and Explore Your Divine Purpose

What's my passion?

1. Complete the following sentence: I'm passionate about the following things . . .

2. How much time do you spend developing these passions? Look back on the past month. How much time did you spend living your passions?

3. When you spend time on your passions, how does it make you feel?

4. Do you feel closer to God when you are spending time on your passions? If yes, why do you think that is so? If not, how do your passions energize the rest of your life?

What's my joy?

1. When was the last time you busted out laughing so hard that you started crying?

2. Describe the last time that you were so excited about doing something that you felt like a little kid.

3. What is it in life that you enjoy doing? Don't be bashful, write down these joys.

4. Why would Jesus say, "I have come that my joy might be in you and that your joy may be full?" When was the last time that your joy was full?

What's my fear?

The first death.

1. Complete the following: The worst way to die would be . . . When I think about my death I feel . . .

2. What are the dreams that you have let die in your life?

3. Does the thought of dying freeze you emotionally and spiritually or does it bring you peace?

The second death.

1. If you don't have a will, get one. If you have a will, what are the most important things that you want to pass on to your heirs? Are there specific material possessions that you want certain people to have? Do these people know your wishes?

2. How do you feel about life-support systems? How long do you want to be sustained by life support?

3. What do you want done with your body when you die? Do you know where you want to be buried or have your ashes scattered? To whom have you made your wishes known?

4. What do you believe happens to your soul after you die? Do you just die and that's it? Does your soul rest until a second coming? Does it step immediately into heaven? Does it pass through several stages? Do you believe that your soul is reincarnated? What has shaped and formed your beliefs about the afterlife?

5. Who are the five people that you most want with you at the time of your death? Why do you want them with you? What do you want to say to them? What will it mean to you for them to be with you at the time of your death? Have you told these people your desire to have them with you when you die? What's keeping you?

The third death

1. How many generations back can you name people from your family? How are certain family members remembered? What are they remembered for? Are they a blessing or a curse?

2. What is the legacy that you want to leave behind? How do you want to be remembered?

3. When do you think will be the last time that your name is mentioned on the planet? For how many generations will your name be remembered?

Fear of not having enough money

1. Are you wearing a pair of golden handcuffs? At what point in your life did those cuffs click into place?

2. Describe any ways that you are already wealthy beyond belief.

3. Who do you know that has the financial "Midas touch"? Are you one of these people? In what ways do all of us have the Midas touch?

4. Given the Parable of the Talents, when it comes to money, which person are you, the person with one, two, or three talents?

5. How can fear and anxiety about money be a root of evil?

6. When you think about your divine destiny, do you often get caught up in the *How's*, as in, "How am I supposed to do this or afford this?"

7. What does this saying mean to you: "When we begin on the way, the way emerges"?

Fear of looking like a fool

1. Describe a time in your life when you had "hoof in mouth" disease. What caused you to say the wrong thing? If you could relive the moment, what would you say differently?

2. Think back to a moment when you looked like a fool. When you think back on that time, what are the feelings that you have? If you could relive that time, what would you do differently? What did you learn from that moment?

3. When was the last time that you had egg on your face? What did you do to overcome the sense of shame?

4. How does the fear of looking like a fool hold you back from stepping out and fulfilling your destiny?

What's my anger?

1. How do you feel about Jesus getting table-flipping mad? Was Jesus justified in his anger? What would happen today if Jesus walked into a church, mosque, temple, or synagogue and began flipping over tables? Would church, mosque, temple, or synagogue members be offended if he did this? Why?

2. When was the last time you were table-flipping mad? How did you express your anger? Were people afraid of your anger? Were you afraid of your anger? What is the difference between being angry and being abusive?

3. Is it all right for you to become angry? Do people allow you to express your anger? How can your anger empower you to action?

4. Make a list of things you are angry about. What about your family? What about your community? Make a list of the issues that make you angry with your church. How about with God? Write them down as well.

Your Gifts

1. List your ten unique gifts, things that you do well—really well. There is only one you and you have particular gifts.

2. How can you be confident of your gifts and at the same time be humble? In what ways do you take your gifts for granted? When was the last time that you deliberately developed your gifts?

3. In what gift have you invested "ten thousand hours"?

4. Who are the trusted people in your life who serve as your editors? Whom do you allow to critique your life, opinions, and actions? Do you receive criticism well? When was the last time someone criticized you? Was it constructive criticism? How did you take that person's feedback?

The Convergence

1. Is there someone in your life who is living his or her destiny? How do that person's answers to questions about passions, joys, fears, anger, and gifts converge into action in his or her life?

2. Try to guess—brainstorm a bit: Where do you see your responses to these questions converging? Where do you see connections overlapping or merging between the different questions?

All the world is full of suffering. It is also full of overcoming.

—Helen Keller

Chapter Six

Sent to Suffer?

In the span of thirty-five seconds, two hundred thousand people die. Their roofs crash on top of them, their walls cave in, gas lines erupt into balls of fire. Their lives are snuffed out like candles on a cake. For those who survive the Haiti earthquake, their homes are reduced to rubble in seconds. Children are suddenly orphaned and parents are left childless. In about half the time it will take you to read this page, the nation of Haiti is destroyed.

An earthquake strikes deep in the ocean floor, and waves rise beyond belief. A tsunami crashes ashore in some of the poorest regions of Indonesia. One hundred fifty thousand people are swept to their deaths, hundreds of thousands left homeless.

Worldwide it is estimated that 7.5 million die of cancer each year. In the United States, cancer kills one thousand five hundred people a day.[1] Six million automobile accidents injure three million people each year. In the United States someone dies of heart disease every thirty-four seconds.[2]

These statistics say nothing about the individuals who have endured these tragedies. When we contemplate cataclysmic events we think of numbers: "one million killed in the Rwanda massacre," "twenty-five million killed by Joseph Stalin," "thousands of children sexually abused." What we forget is that these are people. People with names like Mary, Frank, Betsy, and John . . . humans with skin and bones, thoughts and feelings. They had families, kids, hopes, and dreams. Their existence gets lost in the statistics. These are people, individuals who suffered physical and emotional trauma.

One of the most profound aspects of the Yad Vashem Holocaust Memorial in Israel is the remembrance of the individuals who were murdered by the Third Reich. The average person remembers the number "six million" when thinking of the Holocaust, but Yad Vashem remembers the person. Full-time researchers detail the individual stories of each adult and child, so the person who suffered is never forgotten.

You may be one who is suffering. It may be from an illness, maybe a traffic accident, or maybe your heart was broken because of a divorce or a death. But whatever the cause, the pain wracks your body and grinds dirt into your soul.

Since the existence of suffering is one of the common themes of all religions, it begs the question: Did the Creator send us into the world to suffer? Is suffering a part of the reason we have been sent? Is there something that is expected and desired from our suffering? It is a profound question: How could the Ultimate Being send us into the world to suffer?

A Litany of Suffering

The dichotomy between a loving Creator—who authored our existence, instilled in us a destiny, endowed us with gifts, and sent us into the world—and the presence of accidents, natural disasters, and evil acts is something that has challenged people of faith from the first moment of existence. Theologians have wrestled with this conundrum for centuries.

The Jewish scriptures do not flinch when addressing the complexity of the issue. They are filled with the voices of people who suffer and cry out to HaShem. I imagine the author of Psalm 6 as someone who lost everything. Circumstances have reduced his life to spiritual rubble. Out of his brokenness he writes, "Be gracious to me, O Lord, for I am languishing . . . my bones are shaking with terror. . . . I am weary with my moaning; every night I flood my bed with tears; . . . my eyes waste away because of grief."[3]

I have sat with many people who have endured years of suffering. What felt like a black cloud shadowing them became a dungeon of darkness. In the midst of this despair they felt abandoned. The author of Psalm 22 must have been going through such a time when he wrote, "My God, my God, why have you forsaken me? Why are you so far from helping me, from the words of my groaning?"[4]

Life becomes unbearable when people intentionally seek to undermine or destroy us. Our antagonist might be a family member, a coworker, or even a total stranger. Such a person or persons have devastated the author of Psalm 38: "Those who seek my life lay their snares; those who seek to hurt me speak of ruin, and meditate treachery all day long."[5]

The voice of Psalm 69 speaks for anybody who has been overwhelmed by a flood of financial ruin, a huge tide of grief, or wave after wave of trauma: "Save me, O God, for the waters have come up to my neck. I sink in deep mire, where there is no foothold; I have come into deep waters, and the flood sweeps over me."[6]

If you feel that the Creator is the one who has brought devastation into your life, then you should read the book of Lamentations. The author voices anger, rage, and pain at the suffering he has endured. He is crystal clear who is to blame for this pain: "I am one who has seen affliction under the rod of God's wrath; he has driven and brought me into darkness without any light; against me alone he turns his hand, again and again, all day long."[7] The author compares the Creator to a bear that has torn him apart, and to an archer who has shot an arrow into his gut.[8]

These voices preserved in the Jewish scriptures give credence to the suffering that we all experience. The authors seem to acknowledge the contradiction. On one hand, HaShem is good and faithful and pledges to be with us and protect us; on the other hand, our lives are filled with trauma. How can the one who pledges to protect us allow people to endure everything from torture and rape, to incest and accidents, to calamity and disease? The authors wonder, feel puzzled, and become angered by this God who is good and loving and yet seems helpless against the terrors of life.

Add to this confusion and frustration passages that declare that the Creator has sent us and has a plan for our lives—not just a haphazard plan, but one filled with hope and promise. HaShem says through the Prophet Jeremiah, "I have . . . plans for your welfare and not for harm, to give you a future with hope."[9] Yet as we read the Jewish scriptures we see this divine purpose constantly and consistently thwarted and destroyed through terrible choices and violent actions of individuals and empires. Abel is murdered by his brother Cain.[10] Hagar and Ishmael are sent by Abraham to die in the desert.[11] Dinah is raped,[12] King Saul and his sons are killed in battle,[13] David's son Ammon rapes his half sister Tamar,[14] David has an affair with Bathsheba then murders her husband, Uriah the Hittite.[15] The sword of Joab kills Absalom as he hangs in a tree.[16] Assyrians destroy the Northern Kingdom of Israel and take the people into captivity. The Northern Kingdom of Israel disappears from history.[17] The Southern Kingdom of Judah is overrun by the Babylonians. The Babylonians raze the city of Jerusalem and take many of the inhabitants into exile for seventy years.[18]

These are but a trifling few of the examples of violence and destruction wreaked upon the Hebrew people. The words of HaShem to Jeremiah, "I have plans for your welfare, to give you a future with hope," ring a bit hollow when compared to the very real suffering that people had to endure.[19]

The voice of the Jewish scriptures is not alone; many great theologians through the ages have wrestled with the question, How can a Creator that we call good, loving, omnipotent, all-powerful allow such violence to come into our lives? A Google search turns up hundreds of titles by theologians who have wrestled with this enigma. One theologian, Brian McKinlay, conducted a brief survey of Christian thinking on the topic of why the Ultimate Being allows people to suffer. After explaining the thoughts of the great theologians, McKinlay states, "In response to the sufferer's question, 'Why (is God allowing me to suffer), I am inclined to respond that we simply don't know."[20] Is this true? Is this the way it is? Is it a conundrum that we have to accept, that our suffering may be caused by divine intention? I don't accept it and I encourage you to refuse to, as well.

The Blizzard God

Maybe we have it wrong. Maybe the Ultimate Being does not love us. It could be that the one who created us is as cold as a blizzard. This blizzard God blasts into people's lives with indifference and malice. The blizzard God could blow into our lives, bury us with drifts of pain and anxiety, and blow out again with nary a thought, platitude, or rationale.

Say this with me:

"The Creator does not love."

Do you believe this? I may be able to write it and utter it out loud, but I know it's not true. Love is the core of the Hindu concept of Brahman: "The Lord of Love holds in his hand the world."[21] The Christian concept of God echoes the Hindu teaching: "God is love."[22] For Christians to deny that God is loving denies the reason Jesus was sent into the world: "For God so *loved* the world that he gave his only Son . . . "[23] If God were merely omnipotent, then people might bow down in fear to God, but would they long to have an omnipotent Creator embrace them? An omnipotent embrace feels as cold as a blizzard. An all-powerful Being might be nice, but I don't think I could curl up with this omnipotent Blizzard and share the depths of my soul.

I deeply affirm that the Creator loves us because this is my experience. Beyond what the scriptures of the different religions teach, I feel the Creator's love, embrace, and warmth. I curl up with God like I'm curling up by a woodstove with a good novel on a winter night. I share the longings of my heart like I share my hopes and dreams with my wife. But more than just my romantic notions, I feel the Creator reciprocating this type of presence. God sits with me and listens, ponders, and responds to me.

I can take away many of the Creator's attributes, but if I take away a loving nature, then I'm not so sure that I want this type of Ultimate Being. Even if I am dead wrong and God does not love, I would not bow down and worship an omnipotent Blizzard God.

Why would a person bow down to a being that willfully and intentionally wreaks havoc on human existence? Why would someone bow down to the one who blinked out the lives of two hundred thousand people in an earthquake like switching off so many light bulbs? Why would someone bow down to a God who punishes a person with the hellish pain of AIDS because it disapproved of a certain sexual orientation? I would not bow down to a God like this.

In the same way, even if it meant my neck or the status of my soul, I would not bow down to a human tyrant who hammers people's lives on an anvil of pain and oppression. We have a word for tyrants who wreak holocausts, genocide, and terror upon innocent lives:

Evil

We call them evil. If the Creator is not all-loving then it has the same status as earthly dictators and despots who have oppressed humans through the ages. If this is so, then let me state it clearly: the Creator is evil. If the Ultimate Being is not all-loving, then we don't need a Satan or demons to destroy us; we can lay that blame on the shoulders of the one who created us.

I can't believe I just wrote that.

But it's true. If the Divine Being does not love, then it is evil and should not be worshiped. I would lead the parade away from such a being. I would say burn this book and forget it. You have not been sent, and there is no divine dream for your life. Or, if an unloving deity did send us or had a dream for us, I would say you had better be wary, because it might be a nightmare. I would say be suspicious; don't trust this unloving God, because you would have no idea to what ends you would have been sent.

However, the opposite is true. If there is one thing that I know in the depths of my heart, it is that God is love. One day I walked beside the Sea of Galilee outside the town of Capernaum, where Jesus lived as an adult. A soft breeze blew off the lake; the Bougainvillea splashed brilliant shades of reds, purples, and pinks beside me. I sat on a rock and as I thought about Jesus of Galilee, I was overcome by a divine and holy presence. In that moment I knew in the depths of my being that the Creator *is* love. Jesus taught of God's love and modeled that love. An academic treatise cannot prove this love. It is experienced only in ways that transcend academic processes or articulated rationales. The Creator's love is expressed through measures of the human heart.

Is God Spineless?

There is another way to unwrap this conundrum: Maybe we have the second part of our premise wrong; maybe the Ultimate Being is not all-powerful. If indeed it were an "Ultimate Being," then wouldn't it see, have compassion for, and intervene to alleviate our suffering? What does it say about an ultimate entity who sees but does not respond? There are only so many conclusions that we can draw.

When we must endure caustic cancer drugs, when we watch our children slip through our fingers from leukemia, when we sit beside the bedside of a spouse after a massive stroke, when we pray and pray to God to please intervene . . . and nothing happens, then we must conclude that the Creator either does not love, chooses not to intervene, or is not omnipotent in any way, shape, or form.

If the Ultimate Being created the universe, it would be nice to know that it has some type of power to intervene. I would like to know that it is not helpless against terrorists and tyrants. I would like to know that it is not just a wimp, but actually has some spine. I would like to know that when the Divine Being is backed against the wall it can confront those who dare destroy the creation. However, the history of human suffering is a damning accusation against the Creator's almighty power.

I'll never forget the day I walked through the ovens at Auschwitz. I stood in silence before the eternal flame knowing that hundreds of thousands of faithful Jews came to their death here, many calling to HaShem to save them.

Questions fill my mind as I think of the millions killed by Joseph Stalin. How could a loving creator stand by and allow Pol Pot to simply execute hundreds of thousands of Cambodians? Did the Creator's inaction signify tacit approval when Timothy McVeigh bombed the Alfred P. Murrah building, killing 168 people? Surely the Holy One knew of the detailed plans of the nineteen terrorists who plotted the 9/11 atrocities. If their actions were known but the Creator chose not to intervene, what does that say about the Creator? People of faith are left with few conclusions. Some say in light of such suffering that there is no God. Others say that the suffering is allowed to test our faith. Still others argue that you can't have it both ways—you must choose either an all-loving or an all-powerful nature.

Is there any way out of this? Do we have to choose between the two natures of love and power? When I reflect on my own life and experiences, I have to affirm that the Creator has both of these attributes. I cannot stand on top of fourteen-thousand-foot peaks and gaze down on eagles soaring over mountain ranges and say that the Creator is not all-powerful. I cannot look toward the heavens on a moonless night, at the vast arms of the Milky Way swirling like the dancing arms of a whirling dervish, and know that our planet is but one among billions of stars and planets in our galaxy and our galaxy is but one galaxy among billions of galaxies without affirming in my heart that the Ultimate Being is just that, ultimate.

The Hebrew Psalms declare that power belongs to God.[24] The author of the book of Job describes God's power as thunder.[25] Paul, in the Christian New Testament describes God as full of "great power," a power that not only raised Jesus from the dead but moves through us as well. This power has placed all things under God's rule and authority.[26] Shiva, the Hindu God of destruction and rebirth, embodies a cosmic ultimate power. Shiva is depicted with four arms that are quick and agile. One arm holds a spear that emits lightning bolts.

But more than the scriptures of the Jews or Christian, or the Hindu pantheon, I have experienced the Creator's power firsthand. I have seen this strength fill people with courage to stand tall amidst the pain of impending death. I have seen the divine spirit work through people creating reconciliation in the midst of anger and turmoil. I have felt the sway of the Creator in my own life as I confronted my son's life-threatening illness, shootings that wracked my community, and the deaths of dear friends.

I affirm that the Creator is all-loving and all-powerful. Both are part of the Divine's true essence. It is a puzzle, though, to ponder why there is not more of a direct intervention in our lives to further the divine dream. However, I can't just shrug my shoulders and say, "We simply don't know." I find my answer from the teachings of the Buddha.

Suffering just *is*. It's what the Buddha realized in the moment of his enlightenment. The Buddha's first Noble Truth states it clearly: life is difficult. Humans face hardships not only from disease and illness, but also from forces of nature. People have emotional issues, spiritual longings left unfilled, and hopes and dreams that are dashed by accidents, all of which lead to suffering. I then take this teaching and apply it to my understanding of God. The fact that life is suffering does not negate the love and power of the Creator.

The great insight is that the Creator *does not allow our suffering*. God doesn't passively allow someone to suffer as a tyrant would stand by and allow a slave to be tortured and maimed. The Ultimate Being is not passive in the face of suffering; it actively works to overcome the pain that humans endure, that maybe *you are enduring* as you read this. There is a tremendous divine force that is working to break through your pain. This force is the circumstantial will that I talked about in chapter 2. Whatever your circumstances, this will is working, pushing like the Ganges River, lifting like an elephant to overcome the obstacles you face.

You are not alone.

The Creator is with you. Only someone who has faced death, walked through the depths of depression, felt the stab in the back by enemies, and yet felt a holy presence could have written the Twenty-third Psalm.

This psalm describes HaShem's nurture and comfort. He walks us to meadows and cool waters so we might have rest. But HaShem also has a spine. He has a staff and is not afraid to wield it. HaShem sets a table in the presence of our enemies and invites us to come and eat. As we take a bite, he dares our enemies to bother us. The God of the Twenty-third Psalm brings us overflowing abundance and grace.

God is with us. Psalm 46 repeatedly states that God is with us. God is with us in the midst of natural events that fill us with terror. "Therefore we will not fear, though the earth should change, though the mountains shake in the heart of the sea; though its waters roar and foam, though the mountains tremble with its tumult." God is with us "in the midst of the city," in the midst of our lives. The psalm is adamant: "The Lord of hosts is with us."[27]

While your life may be shattered and reduced to rubble, you must remind yourself that you are not alone. The Creator loves and comforts you. Suffering does not negate a divine presence. Pain is a part of the human condition. We were created with a body that has nerve endings that, when beaten and battered, elicit pain. Life happens, natural events crash into our lives, and evil people seek to destroy us. None of this, however, denies the Creator's presence. In the midst of these circumstances the divine, all-powerful force eventually overcomes the obstacles you're facing. It may take days, months, or even years, but they will be conquered. You may die in the midst of the circumstances you're facing, but the Creator overcomes for your offspring and will prevail.

I Wouldn't, I Don't, and I Won't

It's important to understand the divine role in the wake of natural disasters. When your world collapses because of an earthquake, a tornado, a hurricane, or a tsunami, it is not because you are being punished or your faith is being challenged. Every pastor, priest, or evangelist who says that the Creator sends these cataclysms to punish humanity should be defrocked and never allowed to preach again. The Ultimate Being does not intentionally send suffering to test you. Yes, suffering is a challenge. It pushes you to the edge of your endurance. But our loving and all-powerful Creator does not send us these events to chastise us. Again, why would you want to follow such a God?

I wouldn't, I don't, and I won't.

I wouldn't follow such a God and I wouldn't encourage you to, either. Such a perception makes the Creator a capricious entity that periodically flicks pain on us to see if we are able to endure and still be faithful. In the realm of human justice, this is called abuse. If parents did this to a child they would be arrested and thrown in jail. Why would we ascribe this same kind of behavior to the Creator and somehow deem that it's okay? Let me say it again, the Holy One does not test, try, or punish us with suffering. Suffering is a byproduct of living in a physical world. Suffering just *is*.

The Ultimate Being created the natural world that gives us physics, geology, and meteorology. More than just having been created, it is called good. Our good world includes natural disasters. But this terminology is misleading. From the divine perspective, they are just natural *occurrences*. We are the ones who place a value on them by calling these events disasters.

Humans, caught in the midst of these natural events, experience disastrous consequences, massive property damage and loss of life. So, did the Creator *plan* for these events to happen to us? Only inasmuch as the world was ordered and we were placed in it. These events and our lives, from the divine perspective, are all very good.

When we were sent into the world, the Creator knew that at some point we would coincide with these natural events. When an earthquake destroys lives, it doesn't thwart the divine purpose for our lives. It just means other plans emerge.

Like the instance from chapter 4 when the radiator hose popped, the plan becomes *plans*. True, one cannot compare an earthquake to a radiator hose, but the principle still holds. The earthquake may alter the original dream for you, but as the circumstantial will works, God's multiple plans begin to emerge.

The challenge for you is to resist giving up in the midst of the circumstances. If the Creator is working, then you also must work. Jesus said to the people, "My Father is still working, and I also am working."[28] You must choose to do your part and not give up on God or on yourself. If there is a divine force at work, then you must bring to bear all of your effort as well. As each moment is pregnant with divine potential, you must always strive to discern that potential and choose to embody it with your actions. If your life has been devastated by a natural event, the challenge is to keep your wits about you and ask, "How can I use what is happening to further the sacred purpose of my life? How can I choose for God?" That's easy to say in a book, but it is much harder to say as your car careens out of control and slams into a light pole.

Often we don't have time to think and reflect; we can only choose, act, and respond. In the heat of moments like this I find myself praying, "God choose through me. Place the right action in front of me. Let me respond according to your will." I intentionally try to put on the mind of the Creator so that hopefully I will respond appropriately. We can prepare ourselves for intense moments like this by daily immersing ourselves in the teachings of the Buddha, Jesus, the Tao, and the Bhagavad Gita. Times of meditation and prayer should be part of our daily routine. By dwelling on the divine intention for our lives and seeking each day to embody it, we prepare for these moments. As an emergency room doctor practices and prepares to the point at which the anxious becomes the ordinary, so should we prepare ourselves.

The Ultimate Being created the world to work this way, and we happen to live in this world. It's part of the joy and sorrow of creation.

Still . . . all of this feels like a bunch of hot air.

God's Skin

I can recite fancy theology to describe God's power and love, but that does not alter the fact that a compound fracture causes pain beyond imagination. When children die, the sorrow parents feel rips their hearts. When a mother loses an infant, her grief resembles a primordial echo from the very beginning of existence. While I know that the Creator is with me spiritually, at some point I need more than an ethereal presence. As my young son said to me while I tried to comfort him in the hospital, "Daddy, I want to feel God's skin."

A spiritual presence goes only so far. While we can take spiritual comfort in the divine presence, at some point we need a physical hand to touch us, someone who can actually feel what we feel. We were sent into the world to be a God with skin, to touch those who are suffering.

A major theme of this book is that the Creator works through your life. While God is above us, before us, and around us, God is also uniquely in you, immanent in your existence. The Creator waits for you to choose to act, so that it can then respond to your actions. In a very real way, the power and love of the Ultimate Being are limited by how you choose to respond. It's one thing to say, "God is all-powerful," but if you do not act in the world, then you stifle this power. The same is true for God's love. If I become all flowery about love but do not act in a loving way toward those around me, then really, love is nothing more than my hot air, or as Paul said in the Christian New Testament, "I am a noisy gong or a clanging cymbal."[29]

At a fundamental level, we were sent into the world to physically embody the Creator. As God sent Jesus to be "God with skin on him," so Jesus sends us. Jesus says, "As you have sent me . . . , so I have sent them."[30] We continue not just Jesus's ministry in the world, but God's divine presence. We become divine hands, arms, legs, and mouth.

This is a daunting prospect, because it means that unless we rise up against tyrants who oppress, then the Creator is not all-powerful. If we do not collaborate to give aid to those whose lives have been wracked by natural events, then we limit the divine prerogative. If we do not take the time to sit with those who are suffering, to hold them and care for them, then the Creator is not all-loving. If we do not forgive and work toward reconciliation, then we withhold the divine love.

There is a symbiotic relationship between our actions and the Creator's presence. Theology is nothing more than words about God unless put into action. Books of confessions that spell out doctrines and dogmas about God's almighty power are nothing more than dusty tomes if we don't actually embody this power in the world.

No Child of God Should Cry Alone

Clearly you have been sent into the world. However, your purpose is much more than just fulfilling your potential. You are here to unleash the Creator's divine potential. We have radical free will; we either radically limit or radically liberate God. If you don't act, then the divine potential in the world is not realized. You have been sent to wade into the midst of suffering, sit with those in pain, and hold those who cannot take another step forward. To be a follower of Jesus, Krishna, Buddha, or Mohammed means that you will make every effort to accompany those in tears, that no one should cry alone. While the Creator surrounds us with a comforting, ethereal, holy blanket, it also desires deeply to break through and physically touch us.

You are that breakthrough.

Zakat is one of the pillars of Islam. A literal definition of zakat is "Alms-giving." Faithful Muslims fulfill this pillar by giving a certain percentage of their income to the poor. However, zakat is so much more than money. Zakat is about compassion, mercy, and justice. Zakat motivates a faithful Muslim not just to give alms, but to give of oneself to the community. When a Muslim, motivated by zakat, sits with a mother who has just lost a child, this action makes the love of Allah real. When Muslims work in homeless shelters serving food to those who live on the street, not only are they fulfilling the requirements of zakat, but the presence of Allah radiates through their kind words and acts of encouragement.

Tonglen is a form of Buddhist meditation that eases suffering. To practice tonglen, a Buddhist meditates in such a way as to breathe in the suffering of the world. Then using one's body as a filter, one removes the pain and exhales love, kindness, and compassion. Tonglen can be practiced as a service to the world, but also as a form of healing for an individual. A Buddhist practicing tonglen may sit for hours with someone who is suffering from the effects of chemotherapy. More than inhaling pain and exhaling love, the meditator is surrounding the person with the essence of nirvana. The mediation is exponential. While it may be one person with another, tonglen opens a person to the ultimate feeling of the soul's desire. Nirvana becomes more than just a theory; it is embodied through the one who meditates.

When a Reiki practitioner lays his or her hands on someone who is suffering, heat builds between the palms of the practitioner's hands and the other person's body. The practitioner follows his or her intuition, guided by a spiritual essence. Reiki can be performed on those suffering from a physical ailment, as well as on those who are wrestling with emotional and spiritual stress. The practitioner's hands bring a sense of calm as they move from chakra to chakra. Reiki heals by bringing two people together and allowing for safe touch; but again, it too is exponential. The Reiki practitioner embodies the power of the cosmos. That energy radiates through the practitioner's palms, and the one suffering is put in touch with the cosmic power of the universe.

Zakat, tonglen, Reiki—these are but a few of the practices from the many world religions in which a person puts skin on the divine cosmic presence. What sings from each of these traditions is the notion that through human actions, the Cosmic Being, by whatever name ascribed to it, comforts those who grieve and walks with those who despair.

The Creator has sent you for a divine and holy purpose—to be a divine presence for those who suffer. God is all-loving. God is all-powerful. You are the love. You are that power.

Questions to Help You Discover and Explore Your Divine Purpose

1. Describe a time in your life when you suffered. What caused the suffering? Was it an illness, a person, or an accident? What were the feelings that you had? What does it feel like to remember that time?

2. Who in your life is suffering now? What has caused this suffering? In what area of the world are you most aware of people's suffering? How does this suffering affect you? How does it motivate you to do something?

3. If you had to make a list of the ten greatest atrocities of the past century that caused human suffering, what would they be?

4. Do you believe that God causes humans to suffer? If so, what would God's purpose be?

5. How do you reconcile what God says through the prophet Jeremiah, "I have plans for your welfare, and not for harm, but to give you a future with hope," with the suffering that people experience in their lives?

6. Do you believe that God is all-loving? If so, what does God's love look like? How does it become manifest in the world?

7. Do you believe that God is all-powerful? How does God express this power? Can you believe that God is both all-loving and all-powerful? If so, how?

8. When have you experienced God's love?

9. When have you experienced God's power?

10. Does it bring you any comfort to know that God is with you in the midst of your suffering? If so, how?

11. When was the last time that you sat with someone who was suffering? What did you feel, sitting with them? Was it hard for you? How did you bring comfort to this person?

12. How does our physical presence surround someone who is suffering with the presence of God?

To light a candle is to cast a shadow

—Ursula K. Le Guin

Chapter Seven

Sent as a Scourge?

The Divine Being sent us into the world as lights to brighten the creation. How do some of these lights become blankets of darkness? Does the Creator send people into the world to kill, maim, torture, rape, steal, and vandalize? Is the evil they do the destiny that they were sent to fulfill? It may sound like a silly question, and on the surface the answer is obvious: "Of course not." But if we merely skip over this issue without seriously dissecting it, we miss the profound lesson it teaches.

One argument against the premise of this book is the presence of those whose lives are filled with only hate and destruction: Hitler, Stalin, Pol Pot, Timothy McVeigh, Saddam Hussein, and a host of others. If they were not sent to bring about such evil, where did their ugliness come from? Was some other agency behind their darkness? Did some other force send them to fulfill a destiny counter to God's? If you are to understand the divine light of your purpose, you must also understand those who lurk in its shadow—those who seek to snuff it out.

The Bad Breath of Evil

Evil is not simply an ideological concept. The face of evil in your life is personal. You may be the victim of someone who stomped on your soul with the boot of ugliness.

CHAPTER SEVEN

From white-collar crime to violent rape, evil kicks us around like a mugger in a back alley. Evil has no bias against age, race, nationality, or philosophy. If you are living, it wants to damage or destroy you. Evil is not afraid of crushing children. It is estimated that one in four children has been raped or sexually molested by someone they knew or trusted. The day before I wrote this chapter I was stunned as I listened to a young man in his thirties share his story of being repeatedly raped by a family friend when he was seven years old. He carries the images of the abuse in his mind as a horror film constantly looping in his soul.

Evil especially seeks women to victimize. According to the United States Department of Justice, a woman is raped and abused somewhere in America every two minutes. It is estimated that three million women are physically abused every year in the United States. Globally, there are over three million women and children enslaved. A huge percentage of that number are sold and bought. The U.S. State Department estimates that between six hundred and eight hundred thousand are "trafficked across international boundaries."[1]

The statistics roll like a death march of the damned. While no government admits to endorsing torture, many torment thousands of people every year who dare to speak out, dissent, or question oppressors. The Center for Victims of Torture estimates that five hundred thousand survivors of torture seek to rebuild their lives through their agency.[2] Each of these survivors had someone, another breathing human, break their bones, pull out their fingernails, burn, electrocute, flay, or water board them to either punish them or exact information.

I could go on for pages about bullying in schoolyards, shootings in schools, beatings on college campuses, muggings in inner cities, white-collar crime on Wall Street, and drug cartels in Mexico. As with suffering, the statistics mask the fact that each number represents individual people. Someone, at the hands of others, felt pain that forced them to cower, vomit, and pass out. Many of you reading this book have seen evil face-to-face. You have been mauled by the dark dog, evil. Evil is not some abstract concept. You know it personally; you know its breath.

How can humans, children of God, inflict such pain on other children of God? Maybe that's the problem. Maybe we are not all children of God.

Once when I described a perpetrator of a crime as a child of God, someone shouted at me, "A child of God? The person who beat me was not a child of God. If anything they were the spawn of Satan!" While I understood that his anger was driven by the abuse he had suffered, spiritually and theologically I disagreed.

Christians and Muslims call it Satan. For Hindus it goes by Majapudu. The Buddha knew it as Mara. Call it what you want, this entity is recognized worldwide as a destructive darkness. The question becomes, "How much power does this character have in the world?" Can this darkness spawn violent people and send them into the creation? Can it hold a soul, preknow its destiny, curse people with violent gifts, and fling them into the cosmos? Does it have a plan for certain lives that it guides and shapes to unfold? I don't think so.

I do not believe that this darkness has any creative power at all. Satan's only power is destruction. That is *if* Satan, Majapudu, or Mara exists, and I know many people wrestle with this notion. Arguing for or against its existence goes beyond the purview of this chapter, but if this dark character does exist, then I believe its only power is that of corruption. It lacks one necessary ingredient: it cannot override the free will of any human.

Just as we must collaborate with the Creator to fulfill our divine purpose, we also must collaborate with evil if the dark desires that lurk within the cosmos are to be fulfilled. Ultimately it is not necessary for you to agree or disagree with the existence of old Scratch. We must agree only that for evil to become manifest, humans must *choose* to embody it.

The Evil Choice

The person who molested you as a child *chose* to do it. The person who stole your money and sucked clean your life savings *chose* to do it. They willfully *chose* to go against God's purpose and they *chose* to embody evil. They collaborated with evil, conceived a path of destruction, and fulfilled it.

You and countless millions in the world have lived in the wake of these destructive humans. Their destruction leaves us speechless, pondering, "How could they do this?" Sometimes our only response is simply, "We don't know." I believe differently. I believe we do know how and why people act in evil ways, and we need to examine the problem and name the solution.

Our first question is simply, "Does the Creator send some people into the world to spread violence and mayhem?" Let me be perfectly clear:

No!

The Divine Being has never once held a luminescent soul and planted within that person the purpose of violence and evil. People are not sent into the world to be a scourge upon society. Despots are not born, they are created.

Joy was the intended purpose for every terrorist ever conceived. The Creator held the luminescence of Adolf Hitler's soul and planted the gift of charisma and leadership within him. Stalin, Pol Pot, Osama bin Laden, Timothy McVeigh, Eric Harris and Dylan Klebold, the con man who swindled you, the boss who belittled you, your rapist and molester—all were held in the Creator's palm. They were blessed with gifts and endowed with intentional, circumstantial, and ultimate wills for their lives. There was a divine dream of abundance and the desire that they would bring a great river of compassion into the world.

So what happened?

How did the dream become a nightmare? Some would say that a genetic flaw predisposed them to errant behavior, or that a violent or oppressed childhood created a bully in adolescence and a tyrant in adulthood. Surely there are many times when this is exactly the case. Genetic deficiencies result in violent behavior in young children. Abused children often grow into abusive adults. However, countless other individuals have genetic issues and violent childhoods but choose to counter their past by living compassionate, judicious lives. What is the difference between the two? Is it Satan, Mara, or Majapudu that lures, tempts, and persuades them? It could be. However, the presence of these three does not change the fact that tyrants and bullies willfully choose to embody and perpetuate evil.

Live Spelled Backwards

Evil. That's a heavy word. We shrink from using it. It seems harsh and judgmental. Sometimes, however, it's the only word that describes a despot. It's the best adjective to describe the intentional, willful action of someone who chooses to kill, maim, or torture another human.

In his book *People of the Lie: The Hope for Healing Human Evil*, Scott Peck describes two countervailing forces in the world, a force for life and a force for evil.[3]

Evil is in opposition to life. It is that which opposes the life force. . . .

Evil, then, for the moment, is that force, residing either inside or outside of human beings, that seeks to kill life or liveliness. And goodness is its opposite. Goodness is that which promotes life and liveliness.[4]

Peck makes the fascinating observation that evil is nothing more than l-i-v-e spelled backwards. The simple metaphor captures the essence of the problem. On one hand we have a force moving in the world that propels life. On the other hand, a counterforce moving in the opposite direction propels e-v-i-l.

Our destiny and the divine will—intentional, circumstantial, and ultimate—are a positive force moving through the creation. When we use our free will to embody our sacred purpose, we unleash this positive energy. A tide of love, strength, courage, and joy empowers others. People are inspired by the divine presence in us and they want the same for themselves. They want to experience the joy that we know. Life begets life.

The opposite is also true. People can tragically use their free will to choose against their sacred purpose. If each moment is indeed pregnant with divine possibility, we can choose the exact opposite. We can turn a blind eye to the divine possibility and reject it. Out of hate, spite, revenge, or a myriad of reasons, we can use our free will to unleash a counterforce, a force of evil. It develops its own momentum, unleashing a tide of darkness in others. The evil in one individual pushes another's potential for evil and they too join in a violent current of destruction.

Iris Chang's powerful book *The Rape of Nanking* describes the atrocities committed by the Japanese when they invaded China during World War I.[5] Chang describes how Japanese soldiers raped, bludgeoned, and murdered civilians. While estimates differ, it is believed that more than two hundred thousand Chinese civilians were executed.

When one reads Chang's account of the atrocities, it is frightening to see how soldiers who raped and decapitated people also actively recruited other soldiers to join in the blood bath. Their evil actions unleashed an ugly undertow that sucked others into its vortex. Contests were held to see who could decapitate the most bodies. In mass gang rapes, thousands of women of all ages were violently abused.

Immaculée Ilibagiza, author of *Left to Tell*, describes a similar tide of evil unleashed during the genocide in Rwanda.[6] Hatred swept through the nation as tensions rose between opposing Hutu and Tutsi tribes. In the span of one hundred days, eight hundred thousand people were killed with machetes and axes, often by neighbors who knew their victims. Ilibagiza describes horrific accounts of neighbors encouraging neighbors to join in the hunting and slaughtering of Tutsis. Average citizens became murderers. The force of evil described by Peck moved through Rwanda like a wildfire. The conflagration consumed humans like dead timber.

The perpetrators of this evil were not satanic spawns with horns popping out of their skulls and pointed tails sprouting from the backs of their coats. They did not have genetic flaws; the majority were not abused as children. No, these fellow humans, children of the Creator, *chose* to rape other individuals. Regular soldiers with free will lined up people in Nanking and decapitated them in a killing contest. Normal people in Rwanda who had homes, yards, children, chose . . .

they chose . . .

to exercise their free will, pick up machetes, and hack their neighbors to death. Some might argue that they did not choose, as they were sucked into the mob mentality. I disagree. They may have checked their good sense at the door, but their God-given free will enabled them to wield machetes. They used what the Creator intended for life and chose instead to unleash the counterforce, e-v-i-l.

Stories like Nanking and Rwanda provide specific examples of evil wrought by humans. Any student of history can recall similar atrocities perpetrated against Jews in the Holocaust, citizens of Cambodia, or Native Americans of the United States. You have examples from your own life of people who have bullied, beaten up, and terrorized other individuals.

Yet the perpetrators of this violence are not demonic monsters; they are people like you and me. The chilling truth is that each of us has the ability to unleash this same tide of evil. Each of us has the same potential to misuse our free will and become a scourge upon society.

The Creator's dreams for Hitler, Pol Pot, a Japanese soldier, or an ordinary Hutu have the same framework as ours. God held the luminescence of their souls, planted a destiny, bestowed gifts upon them, and flung them along a certain life trajectory. As in all lives, these people were shaped by their own circumstances. But at some point they *chose*. They made deliberate decisions to cross a line. They chose to pervert a blessing, to curse the world.

Baby Steps

The Buddha, in the Dhammapada, taught, "Let no man think lightly of evil, saying in his heart, 'It will not come nigh unto me.' Even by the falling of water-drops a water-pot is filled; the fool becomes full of evil, even if he gather it little by little."[7] This drip, drip, drip that the Buddha describes is what I call baby-stepping your way into evil.

People rarely take one gigantic action and become murderers, tyrants, or thieves. If they do, usually these people are quite easy to rehabilitate back into health. Their violent action is such an aberration from their normal behavior that with the right therapy they can be restored to wholeness. Truly evil people, however, are completely different. They have fallen so slowly into dark ways that their present condition feels as ordinary as taking a dog for a stroll.

Dan was stunned when he was convicted of fraud. He was sentenced to several years in jail and faced restitution of hundreds of thousands of dollars. Dan's life had left a wake of ruin for the people who had trusted him with their financial well-being. Many of Dan's clients are now destitute, as their retirement savings vaporized with his financial schemes. Dan developed an elaborate Ponzi scheme that, while at first generated great returns, eventually imploded on Dan, his family, and his clients.

Dan had strong financial acumen. He graduated with honors from a prestigious university with a degree in finance. Dan immediately found a job with an investment firm and made a handsome salary. When he went to work he felt as though he had found his emotional home. He loved making money, and he loved helping people develop financial security.

But Dan's brilliance had a dark side. It wasn't long before Dan realized that he could skim a profit from each business transaction for his own ends. Slowly, day-by-day, Dan was accumulating a small fortune. However, other financially bright people in the firm began to notice inconsistencies in Dan's accounting. Dan was confronted, and it was agreed that if Dan paid back what he had stolen from the company, he would simply be released from the firm and no charges would be filed. Dan was embarrassed and insisted that he had not really done anybody any harm, but agreed to take the settlement and leave.

Faced with unemployment, Dan turned to what he knew, finance. He set up an office in his home and began using his charm and personality to influence people to allow him to invest their money. All it took was one client. Dan used his skills to invest the money with great returns. The pleased client gave Dan's name to a trusted friend, who was also very happy with Dan's ability. This client referred Dan to other friends and the ball began rolling. Soon Dan's name was mentioned in social circles as someone to go to for investment strategies. Over two years Dan developed quite a clientele who wanted him to invest their money. Dan not only returned huge financial rewards to those who entrusted their money to him, but was able to purchase a beautiful home, an expensive car, and vacations abroad. From all appearances, it looked as though Dan had landed on his feet.

But behind the scenes of Dan's life, things were slowly deteriorating. Client-by-client, Dan had devised a financial scheme that was nothing more than a straw house. With each new client he recruited, Dan built a façade of success from which he personally benefited. As the façade grew taller, it began to sway, ready to collapse and crush those who trusted him.

Things went exceedingly well for Dan until the national economy soured and people wanted their investment capital returned. But their investments had been used to pay other investors. It happened quickly: Dan was investigated, the scheme was discovered, and Dan was taken from his house in handcuffs. His investors were bilked of millions. Retirees lost their life savings. College funds evaporated, and people lost their homes. Dan's scheme had wreaked havoc and ruin on hundreds of people who trusted him and his gifts.

Dan didn't kill anybody. He didn't pick up a machete and behead anyone. He didn't rape any women, and he never held a knife to someone's throat. But what he did was evil. He took the gift the Creator gave him and chose to use it for destructive ends.

When contemplating examples of evil for this chapter, I felt it would be too easy to tell the stories of a drug dealer, a murderer, a political tyrant, a Hitler, stepping daily into evil. It's easy to hear such a story and say, "I'm not that person." But Dan's story is fairly ordinary and common. While I changed his name, "Dan" is an actual person whose clients, people I know, were left destitute.

If not Dan, I could have used example after example from everyday life. I could have told you about Martha, the stay-at-home mother who destroyed others' reputations through gossip. Or Mark, a talented artist whose lies and deceit wrecked people's lives like a locomotive jumping from its tracks. Or I could have described Bill, the oppressive boss who enjoyed bullying his employees.

The point is that anybody can embody and perpetrate evil. The point of a pen, the tip of the tongue, the lash of an emotion, is just as sharp as the edge of machete when it comes to evil. If Dan could fall prey to evil actions so can you and I.

It's a daily challenge to choose for the force of life. If we don't actively choose for life, we actively choose for evil. You can't be neutral. Your life is going in either one direction or the other. As Moses said to the children of Israel in the Jewish scriptures, "I have set before you life and death, blessing and curses."[8] You have to choose which way your life is headed.

The greater challenge is to understand that the two opposing forces are not on a level plane. If good and evil could be put on a continuum, with life moving in one direction and evil moving in another, the force of life would point uphill. To choose your divine purpose, the reason you were sent, is often the greater, uphill challenge. On the other hand, to choose for evil is to follow a greased path by which you can easily slip and slide into darkness. To choose for good often takes reflection, introspection, and evaluation. Choosing for the divine bias in a particular situation requires you to step back from a knee-jerk reaction and reflect on the Creator's purpose. You have a say-so; take a moment and think, What actions further your divine dreams and desires? Choosing the good requires us to evaluate our own behavior so that we are not perpetrating evil ourselves. Choosing for good is a challenge. It's difficult work.

Choosing evil, however, is as easy as flicking a fly from your arm. Evil basks in quick and impulsive actions. If someone cuts you off in traffic, you flip them off and drive on. If someone strikes out at you, you devise a punishment that not only inflicts the same pain you felt, but teaches that person to never mess with you again. At first you may struggle with acting on violent impulses, but eventually, you become accustomed to it. You become hardened and no longer think anything is wrong with what you are doing. You have been doing it for so long that it feels normal. You have baby-stepped your way into evil.

The Ember That Always Glows

Even so, the Holy One never abandons someone who chooses evil. If the psalmist is right that HaShem is with us, then he is with those who rape, belittle, and destroy. He is with those who oppress and steal. The divine circumstantial will is still active, still trying to pull the individual back toward life and health.

Like a frog in a pot of water slowly brought to a boil, some people become immersed in evil. The light of love inside them becomes all but smothered. But the fact that a blanket covers a fire doesn't mean that the embers don't smolder in the ashes. The Creator is still present in the vilest of human beings. Divine love is still there, hoping, luring, and using every ounce of power to bring the person to the force of life. The Lord Krishna in the Bhagavad Gita[9] says to Arjuna, "Even the heartless criminal, if he loves me with his whole heart, will certainly grow into sainthood as he moves toward me on this path." The key to the criminal attaining sainthood, however, is the person's free will.

Just as Majapudu cannot override our free will, neither can the Supreme Being. As I have said earlier, our free will is the hairball in the grand design. The metaphor describes the potential mess that we can make in the cosmos. One wrong move and we can spend our lives spinning out of control. A lifetime of wrong choices can push millions of people to their deaths.

It's up to you and me to choose what kind of tide we unleash in the world around us. We can live like an unchained rabid dog wreaking the force of evil, or we can be playful Labradors bounding with love and joy—the force of life. The Creator has left it up to us to choose.

The Skid Mark on the Soul

Imagine someone smacking you and knocking out one of your molars. You then plot your revenge. You want to take pliers, kneel on the jerk's chest, grip a tooth, and yank it out by its roots—a tooth for a tooth. The desire for revenge festers like a boil on your soul. The danger is that when you stoop to revenge, when you want the payback, you embody the evil that you hate. The Satan you don't believe in then laughs at how, through your piety, you become the avenue by which Satan's dank seed grows. But then, how do you respond to evil? Are you just a doormat? Do you turn the other cheek while evil people walk all over you? No, but the challenge is to learn how to respond.

Evil is like black tar. Have you ever stepped in hot tar? Not only does it burn the soles of your shoes, it gets all over you. Everywhere you step you leave a trail of black goo. If you try to scrape it off with your hand, it smears on your skin. Then when you wipe your hand on your jeans, it ruins the denim. Throw the jeans in the washer and the tar gums up the motor and turns the other clothes black. There is no easy way to clean off tar. In the same way, there is no easy way to deal with evil.

People respond to the black tar of evil in many ways. Some people cower, others flee, and some become filled with rage and strike back. Striking back is like sticking your hand in a bucket of tar. The evil sticks to you, sucking you into its ugliness, smearing your life like a black skid mark of despair. When you strike back at evil you unwittingly respond with your own evil actions. Your motivation may be righteous, but as with the Christian Crusaders of old, your desire to stamp out evil opens the gates of ugly actions that leave the stain of blood on your own hands.

There is only one way to respond to evil, and that is with love, compassion, and forgiveness. The Christian New Testament teaches, "See that none of you repays evil for evil."[10] The Buddha taught, "For hatred can never put an end to hatred; love alone can."[11] These teachings provide the only sane way to respond. By returning evil with compassion and love, you break the cycle of action and reaction and keep your soul aligned with the force of life. Forgiveness is one of Jesus's most profound teachings. Jesus taught to have forgiveness rooted in your being. You are to practice forgiveness in every corner of your life. This mirrors the Creator's forgiveness of us.

However, you may refuse to forgive someone because you just don't understand how to do it. You think that if you forgive someone, you have to let that person back into your life. If you extend forgiveness you have to forget what happened. You think forgiving is a quick statement, "You're forgiven," and everything is smoothed over. None of these are true. Forgiveness is a long, slow process. Abusers are not allowed back into your life. Nor do you let them go scot-free; they are held accountable for their actions. You don't forgive and forget; instead you remember who they are and what they did. In the process you cleanse yourself of the bile that has built up in your soul.

The process of forgiveness involves remembering exactly what happened to you.[12] As you remember, though, you give up the right to get even. While you may feel that striking back is just and appropriate, in the process of forgiveness you realize this action/ reaction cycle is nothing more than sticking your hands in the bucket of tar. Returning evil for evil is reversing your path, striding in the exact opposite direction from what you are working to embody. Forgiveness is a process through which you invite the Creator's presence into your heart and life to heal your brokenness and pain. The ultimate goal of the process of forgiveness, which may take years, if not a lifetime, is to wish someone well in life, thus releasing the person from the emotional hold he or she has on you.

Ultimately, forgiveness boils down to a choice. When someone blasts your life off the divine trajectory, remember that you have a choice. You may want to say that the knee-jerk reaction of responding to evil with rage is only normal. If so, you miss the point of free will. Nothing is knee-jerk. If you have a knee-jerk reaction to something, it's because that reaction has become a habit. This pattern doesn't negate the fact that you still have a choice. God gave you the ability to choose. When someone does you evil, you can unleash your own tide of evil, or you can choose to practice forgiveness, love, and compassion. When you aspire to these higher virtues, you are embodying your destiny at its most profound level. You have been sent into the world to break a pattern of evil in your life and begin a completely new and different legacy; this is what the Supreme Being sent James to do.

Generations of Violence

James's story is one of heartbreak and pain. His father physically abused him and his siblings throughout their childhood. Their lives were filled with fists, straps, and bruises. After James had been married for years and started raising his own children, he realized he needed to see a therapist. It took many years of hard work for James to unpack the violence that he had lived through. James began to realize that from generation to generation, as far back as he could find, children in his family had been violently physically and sexually abused. James's ancestors left a foreboding shadow of violence that his father had visited upon him. He described it as a black pall hanging over his family. He had pictures of his ancestors in the hallway of his house, but took them all down as they represented traditions not of hope and joy, but of abuse and sorrow. Every time he went down that hallway he had felt as if he were walking death row.

The reason James came to see me was that he felt as though the Creator had given him a message he wanted to understand. He was told that he had been sent into the world to stop the legacy of abuse. James believed that his life's purpose was to confront the violence of his family, learn to forgive his father, and create a new legacy of hope and joy. He asked me if I believed that God acted in this way, that God sent people into the world for purposes such as this.

"Yes," I told James, "I do believe that the Creator sends people into the world with just such intentions." After the long conversation that followed, James realized that he had a choice. He could choose to blindly bury the pain of what had been done to him, or he could live intentionally with his family and create a new legacy with his own wife and children. He realized that he wasn't forced along this path, but that the Creator was waiting for him to join in creating something new. James was able to forgive. He struggled to do the hard work that kept him on the path of life. James was sent by the Supreme Being to break a history of violence and to usher in a whole new era for his family—a life of hope.

Mirror Neurons

Jeremy Rifkin, in his book *The Empathic Civilization*, explains that humans have mirror neurons wired into their brains.[13] When someone sees another person experiencing happiness, joy, pain, and even anger, the neurons "mirror" the same feeling. Through these mirror neurons people can feel and identify with someone else's experiences. Rifkin argues that what neuroscience and neuropsychology are teaching is that instead of being wired for anger, aggression, and self-interest, our brains are wired for sociability, attachment, affection, and companionship. Our brains are wired for empathy. It's a part of our makeup. As you grow and mature from childhood through adolescence into adulthood, you have the innate ability to empathize with someone else's plight.

Since the cosmic electrician wires empathy into you, you have compassion; it's the divine purpose for you at its deepest level. When the Creator held the luminescence of your soul and planted within you your gifts and destinies, you were also given the desire to be empathic. It was part of the design from the dawn of creation. You were sent into the world to identify with the plight of others. When you are with people who are suffering, you can feel their suffering in your body and respond in such a way that you become God with skin.

On the other hand, your mirror neurons enable you to experience the darkness of evil, not only in others, but also in yourself. If you are in the presence of someone who embodies evil, your mirror neurons allow you to experience your own rabid dog. The other person's dark dog touches the dark dog that lurks within you. With our neurons firing away, the consummate challenge is to refrain from responding to evil with evil. We must keep the dog leashed. We need to learn how to pause, recall the teachings of the scriptures, and choose the uphill journey of life.

James allowed his mirror neurons to move him to a place of compassion. He felt in the depths of his being the horror of what had been done to him by his father. As his therapy progressed he was able to empathize with his father, who had suffered his own abuse at the hands of James's grandfather. James felt his father's suffering deep within his own body. Like a dawn beginning a new day, the understanding came to James that he could choose between evil and life. He chose for life. The Creator had sent James, but it was up to James to choose.

You are wired in such a way that you feel what other people feel in their bodies. If someone is suffering, you can feel it in your own muscles and bones. If someone is laughing, it promotes laughter in you; you can empathize with their joy and long to feel it yourself. The same is true with evil.

In the midst of the trauma that evil people wreak in the lives of others, their terror echoes in your own soul. This is why people feel nausea and rage in the midst of evil, as they realize they, too, could suffer the same pain. As the mirror neurons spark, constantly remember that you always have a choice: return evil for evil, or life. As the Creator sent James to begin a legacy of hope and joy, so have you been sent. You are sent to unleash a force of life. It all depends on what you choose to do.

Questions to Help You Discover and Explore Your Divine Purpose

1. Does God send some people into the world for evil purposes?

2. Who are the great despots of the past century? Would you call these people evil? Why, or why not?

3. How have you been a victim of evil? Who has done these things to you?

4. Do you believe in Satan? If not, why not? If you do, where do you believe Satan came from?

5. Does Satan send people into the world? Is there such a thing as a spawn of Satan?

6. What is the difference between human evil and satanic evil?

7. Why do you think people choose to act in evil ways?

8. Describe someone that you know who is embodying a force of life. Describe what that person's life looks like.

9. Who is someone you know who is embodying evil? What does that person's life look like?

10. Describe a time in your life when you sank your arm into a "bucket of tar" and unintentionally smeared yourself with the muck of revenge?

11. How does forgiveness keep you from sinking your arm into the bucket of tar?

12. What was the hardest thing that you ever had to forgive? Where are you in this process?

13. What have you done that you have had to be forgiven for?

14. Which is harder, to forgive someone else or to forgive yourself?

God has made us so that we will need each other.

—Desmond Tutu

Chapter Eight

Sent Together

Seven billion. Seven billion humans are tramping around this planet. I find this number stunning. This means that the Creator has preknown seven billion souls; planted a destiny within them, blessed them with gifts, and sent them into the world. Here we all are. Like a billion swarms of ants, flies, and bees; like a billion flocks of swallows and finches dancing in the air, we are all teeming on the surface of the globe.

Here *you* are, one in seven billion. Out of all of these billions, the Cosmic Being has singled you out. You are special, loved, and empowered. You have been sent to do something unique. However, there's more to it than just fulfilling your destiny alone. From the perspective of the world's great religions, you are to collaborate with others to create something grand.

Imagine this with me: there is something wonderful about a symphony with seven billion instruments. What about a sports team with seven billion members or a dance troupe with seven billion dancers? Now you may be thinking that this could be a cacophony of noise and chaos. But the Creator perceives something very holy about seven billion people working together. It was the cosmic design from the very beginning.

In the Jewish religion, it begins with Adam. HaShem created Adam and realized that it was not good that he was alone, so Eve was created. When HaShem decided to create a special people, he called Abraham and Sarah together. When the children of Israel were imprisoned in Egypt, HaShem sent Moses and Aaron together to set the people free.

In the Hindu faith there are many stories and legends of the holy pantheon collaborating to solve the problems of the world. Krishna cooperates with Vishnu. Vishnu and his wife, Lakshmi, brainstorm together to address problems that confront humans. Each of these gods uses unique powers to collude and conspire to further the progress of the world.

In the Christian New Testament, when Jesus started his ministry the first thing he did was to gather a group of twelve disciples. When Jesus sent the disciples on their first mission he sent them out in pairs. Paul and Barnabas went to spread the good news together. There is something about teams of people working together, collaborating, brainstorming, and implementing their ideas, capturing the essence of the Creator's intentions for us.

Jesus said, "Whenever two or three are gathered in my name, there I am among them."[1] It's a holy thing when two people come together. When two hearts open and connect, when two minds expand and share, when two bodies work side by side, it's more than just two people. A third entity is present—the spirit of the Supreme Being. So if this sacred dynamic is present when two or more are gathered, what is the effect when seven billion congregate? It has to be a holy chorus.

The Religious Chickens at the Feed Trough

But if it's such a holy chorus, why is collaboration so hard? I have always held a personal corollary to Jesus's teaching: "Whenever two or more are gathered in Christ's name, there's bound to be a fight."

People of faith, children of God of all brands, can't seem to agree on anything. As a pastor I have seen some bitter disputes, often over trivial issues such as styles of music, placement of flowers, and who gets which space in the church building. And it's not just my particular church. People of all religions fight and squabble like chickens at a feed trough. There are thousands of religions in the world; there are hundreds of splinter groups within each religion; Christians are the worst—according to Adherents.com there are over thirty-eight thousand different Christian denominations.[2] Read that again . . .

thirty-eight thousand

It's a staggering number. Thirty-eight thousand Christian denominations created by splits, conflicts, and disagreements. It's sad. If Christians, who by their very nature and creation are supposed to collaborate but can't, or won't, what does that say for the rest of the world?

The Creator intends that we work with one another. We are sent together. For your dream to be fulfilled, you have to learn how to join forces with seven billion other people. While I have encouraged you to discover your personal dream, it's not really about you. It's about us working together, collaborating, sharing, working through conflicts and differences, overcoming boundaries (real and imagined), and empowering one another so that the divine purpose for all of creation is realized.

Ubuntu

The Africans call it *ubuntu*. This may be a new term for you, but it provides the vision that we need to adopt if seven billion of us are going to not only get along, but accomplish something grand for God.

Ubuntu connotes community. But more than just community, it's a way of living together and collaborating by which the uniqueness of each individual is realized through interdependent relationships. In the Western world, identity and meaning are found when individuals discover their gifts and express them through a job or a career. Conversely, ubuntu reasons that individuals discover their true uniqueness only by being in an interdependent relationship with others. Archbishop Desmond Tutu used the concept of ubuntu to create a powerful vision of inclusion that eventually brought down the system of apartheid. Tutu states, "To be is to participate. The summum bonum[3] here is not independence, but interdependence."[4] When people come together and collaborate in a trusting communal setting, other members of the community validate their participation and recognize their uniqueness. Tutu adds that ubuntu "asserts that persons are ends in themselves only through the discovery of who they are in others. For example, one cannot recognize one's own physical beauty unless another person is present who can reveal or reflect that beauty."[5] Ubuntu recognizes that we have been interdependent from the moment of our birth.

Tutu's vision of ubuntu is that our differences are critical for the strength of the community. We need one another's complementing gifts and skills. Our differences are valued. The ubuntu vision is to create communities of trust where people can be vulnerable with each other and express their deepest thoughts and desires, knowing the community listens and honors them.

Ubuntu is a compelling concept, but it is very challenging to create. Encouraging and empowering teams of people to come together in a spirit of ubuntu is one of the greatest mysteries of management. Some teams work together in such a way that their collaboration is a magnificent reflection of the Creator's presence. There are also plenty of examples in which management teams and interfaith groups have been angry, contentious, and openly destructive. If you have ever led a group, if you're a manager, a supervisor, if you are a part of a religious group, then invariably you too have experienced the bitter fights that break out among those who claim to be children of God. If Tutu is correct that interdependence is a part of our divine identity, one would think it would be a little easier to create and experience.

Russell Linden, a management consultant and author, in his book *Leading across Boundaries: Creating Collaborative Agencies in a Networked World*, contends that while collaboration is a necessary part of the human experience, it rubs directly across the grain of our Western culture.[6] We are so deeply steeped in our rugged individualism that we have forgotten how to come to the table and work together. This is tragic. Our desire for individualism has yanked us from the deep moorings of our creation. We were created to work together, yet not only have we forgotten how, but in some cases we have no desire to do so.

As someone who has been sent into the world, you must learn how to embody the ubuntu vision. Your divine destiny is realized only as you are able to overcome obstacles and learn new skills in concert with others. As you empower people to embody their divine destiny, you are then empowered. You and seven billion other people must learn how to come together and collaborate. Quite the challenge, isn't it? However, after spending my career working with groups of people, I believe it is possible when you have the desire to join others to fulfill what the Creator sent you all to do.

Linden suggests that, while collaboration is complicated and exasperating at times, only a few basic impediments stand in the way: ego, turf wars, information silos, and the fear of losing control. Let's look at each of these challenges.

Ego

As someone sent into the world, you must learn how to check your ego at the door.[7] While you have been sent to fulfill your purpose in life, your destiny is ultimately about fulfilling the divine desire for the world. If your only focus is to have your needs met, your vision accomplished, your ideas presented, then you have missed the reason you were sent in the first place. Yes, you have been given unique gifts. But if this makes you puffed up and full of yourself, you will never be able to collaborate with anybody to accomplish a far greater purpose.

There is a tension between confidence and humility. Confidence helps you overcome fear and moves you out of your comfort zone. Humility comes from the Creator and keeps you grounded.

Bob had a huge ego, which made it impossible for people to work with him. He was a big person with a loud voice and an energy that filled a room. At first people were attracted to Bob's sparkling personality. However, after working with him for a few weeks, people discovered that his sparkles were just rhinestones Bob wore on the crown of his ego. It was not just that Bob knew he was sent by God, but he seemed to also believe that he was God's great gift to the cosmos. In meetings, Bob demanded that things be done his way. He constantly fished for compliments. He would pout when the group disagreed with him. Bob would push and push against the group's desire until people caved in to his agenda out of the sheer desire to shut him up. It was impossible to collaborate with Bob because his ego was constantly in the middle of the bargaining table.

Bob's destiny will be realized only if he learns how to check his ego at the door. While the world needs what Bob has to offer, he has to realize that he needs what every other person brings to the table as well.

When Jesus said, "Whenever two or more are gathered," he didn't mean you and your ego. To realize the joy of collaborating you must come to terms with yourself. Look in the mirror and be honest with yourself: Do you have to grease your ego to get it through a doorway? Do you fish for compliments as if you were in a bass derby? In your mind's eye, are people constantly giving you a standing ovation? If so, your ego is getting in the way. Your purpose and destiny will not be realized if you feel as though your agenda has to be the driving force of the group's process.

At the heart of an inflated ego is fear. People who constantly need to be recognized for their accomplishments are acting out of the fear that they will be ignored. Somewhere in their childhood or adolescence, they decided that the only way they could receive affirmation was to overstate their presence. Maybe they were skilled in a particular area, but ultimately they were afraid that their abilities did not measure up, that they were going to be overlooked, or that when compared with others they would be found lacking or fraudulent. To cover their fear they overstated their case. When challenged on their skills they became combative and competitive. When ignored they sulked, became cynical about the group's ability to carry on without them, and learned to pick up their gifts and go home. To assuage their need to be recognized, others acquiesced, overpraised, and cast too many spotlights on these needy people. The behavior becomes a pattern that over a lifetime can grow to become an inflated ego.

Your ego needs to be grounded and strengthened, not in your own ability, but in your gifts from the Creator. Your sense of confidence comes from knowing that a far greater power entrusted you with these talents for the betterment, not only of your personal life, but of every person on the planet. Your expertise should not puff you up, but instead create a deep sense of humility. Knowing that you have been entrusted with these skills should bring you to the communal table humbly offering what the Creator gave you. Your gifts are not the be-all and end-all, but are unique and critical parts of a group project. Instead of fear, you should be motivated by a humble confidence that the Divine Being's presence works not only in you, but also with each person gathered together.

Turf Wars

Turf wars are the second great impediment to collaboration.[8] Turf, soil, ground, lawn—we fight to control our real estate. Gangs claim neighborhoods as their turf. Nations set up boundaries and claim the land within them as their turf. Businesses claim certain products and consumers as their turf. Religions passionately defend their path to God as their turf. We set up our own emotional boundaries as our turf and dare anyone to trespass against us.

Churches are notorious arenas for turf defenders. I have seen churches self-destruct as people fought over petty disagreements. Turf wars are nothing more than the hand saying to the foot, "I have no need of you." Those who guard their turf have no concept of what the apostle Paul means when he states in the Christian New Testament that we are a body that needs each part.[9] The concept of turf is completely absent in the ubuntu vision.

Let me be clear: you were not sent into the world to guard some piece of turf. The Divine Being did not preknow you and give you gifts so that you could protect some piece of real estate—physical, spiritual, or imagined. If the world's problems are ever going to be solved, the solutions are going to come from people willing to let go of their turf. People will have to overcome their national identities, business affiliations, and religious biases. They will have to take down the fences protecting their turf and invite people over for barbecue and potato salad. They have to learn how to collaborate so that everyone's turf grows green and fertile.

Jesus tells a parable about turf: Once a landowner planted a beautiful vineyard and built a wall around it. In the middle of the vineyard he built a winepress so that the grapes could be made into a wonderful wine. The landowner planned to make a huge profit when the wine was sold. After the vineyard was planted, the walls were finished, and the winepress stood tall, the owner went to a distant country and left the gardeners in charge. When it came time to harvest the grapes, create the wine, and sell the product, the owner sent servants back to receive the profit. When the gardeners saw the servants coming, they beat them severely, wanting to keep the profits themselves. The owner continued to send servants, thinking that eventually the gardeners would come to their senses and give the landowner his rightful due. But each servant, upon arriving at the garden, was beaten senseless and kicked out of the garden. Finally the owner sent his son, thinking that surely these gardeners would listen to him. Instead they said, "This is the heir, let us kill him, then surely the vineyard will be ours!" So they killed the son and kicked his body outside the vineyard walls. After telling the story, Jesus asked, "What do you think the owner of the vineyard will do? Right! He'll come and clean house! Then he'll assign the care of the vineyard to others."[10] When you guard your emotional, spiritual, religious, or ideological turf, you are like the gardeners who beat the servants and killed the son. As someone sent into the world, you are the gardener that God has left in charge of the vineyard, the grapes, and the winemaking. The profit does not belong to you, but to the one who sent you. Instead of guarding your grapes within the walls of the vineyard, it is expected that you will openly engage with others, not only selling the product but also sharing the bounty.

The ubuntu vision of this parable is that the gardeners would see that they need everyone to be part of the winemaking: the servants, the wine merchants, the son, and the landowner. Each person is an interdependent part of the process. The Creator is the landowner, you are the gardener, and the vineyard is the community where you live. You were sent to work in this vineyard, collaborating and sharing the bounty with the world. To guard your turf, to threaten, beat, and kill anyone who trespasses, angers the one who created the vineyard in the first place.

Fear is the root motivation for those who guard their turf. Individuals guard their property, their ideas, and their gifts when they are afraid they won't receive what they think they are due. Religious groups guard the turf of their ideology, fearing they will be polluted by differing systems of belief. Church, synagogue, and temple members guard their buildings, budgets, and worship style because they are afraid their sacred beliefs will be lost. Businesses guard the turf of their products because they are afraid that the competition will steal their ideas. Nations guard the turf of their boundaries, fearing the influx of immigrants will jeopardize their economy and political systems. Our fear keeps us hemmed inside the walls of our vineyard and runs counter to the intent of the landowner who sent us to work here.

When you guard your turf you're acting out of a scarcity mentality. You are afraid that there will not be enough of what you hold sacred. So you hoard, build walls, and arm yourself to keep out anyone who threatens what is special to you. A scarcity mentality runs completely counter to the abundance of the world. As a person sent into the world, you need to know that there is an abundance of ideas, thoughts, and products to be exchanged and sold with others.

Are you are guarding some turf? Is it market share, a specific idea or thought, a tradition, a family distinction, a business concept that you feel is inherently yours? As you march around the boundaries of your turf, what would happen if instead of looking for the enemy you were searching for someone to collaborate with? Instead of turf, you would find a green lawn of abundance to share with others.

Silo Mentality

Similar to guarding your turf is developing a silo mentality. Russell Linden describes a silo mentality as hoarding ideas, creativity, and information for fear that sharing them would give someone else a competitive edge.[11]

Imagine a silo standing tall in the midst of a cornfield. It's filled with grain that can feed thousands of people around the world. Its purpose is to store the goods so they can be disseminated and shared. What good is a silo if the grain sits and rots? Nothing—its purpose is wasted.

The Buddha taught about silo mentality. He told a jataka about a previous lifetime when he was incarnated as the chief justice of a town.[12] He was faced with two angry merchants standing before him, one from the country and one from the city.

When the country merchant came to the city he stored his materials in the city's warehouse and went about his business. When the city merchant saw the goods stored in his building he became jealous and wanted them for himself. So he took the items, placed them in a secret holding cell, and then spread mouse dung on the floor. When the country merchant returned and found that his goods had disappeared, he asked his friend what had happened. The city merchant told him that while he was gone, mice came and ate all of the goods. "I'm so sorry," said the city merchant, "but it is the way things are." The country merchant was puzzled but shrugged his shoulders and went to the river to bathe. On the riverbank he found the son of the city merchant, took him, and hid him in another person's house. When the city merchant came to the river looking for his son, the country merchant said, "While your son was bathing a hawk came and swept him away. I'm so sorry; it's just the way things are." The city merchant was outraged and yelled, "Murderer! You have murdered my son!" The two then appeared before the local chief justice, who was the incarnation of the Buddha. The judge heard the case and saw the guile in the city merchant and ordered that the goods be restored to the country merchant, and only then would his son be returned.

The teaching is clear: hoarding goods not only is selfish, but it leads to destructive karma that disrupts community life. The scarcity mentality leads to envy and the desire to steal. An action/reaction cycle was created in which the two merchants, instead of collaborating, were pitted against each other. The relationship of trust they initially established was destroyed by the city merchant's desire to steal from the country merchant.

The Buddha's presence in the midst of the story presents a deep spiritual ethic for the way we share our resources. The Buddha is not just in the temple or under a Lotus tree, but present in each of our daily transactions. The way we approach our business relationships reflects our spiritual connections.

The purpose of having a wealth of information is to spread out your ideas. The reason you have creativity is to engage with others. Your passion, your sharp mind, and your ability to teach, work on automobiles, explore the innards of a molecule, or manage people are for the benefit of the world. If you hoard your ideas, you are like the city merchant spreading mouse dung around your boardroom. You can't meditate with the Buddha on Tuesday evening and then forget about his teachings on Wednesday morning as you open your business doors. Your faith and your life must be integrated.

Imagine seven billion information silos hoarding information. The world would choke and die from the lack of creativity. Sadly, the knowledge to feed the world is right at your fingertips. You can participate in the feast if you are willing to open your silo and share what the Creator sent you to do.

What creates a silo mentality? Fear and scarcity are the structures of information silos.

Are you sensing a theme here?

We are motivated by fear. We protect our turf, build walls, and fill our silos because we are afraid.

Wes had a silo mentality. He was a brilliant computer programmer and had many exciting ideas about software design. But he felt threatened by anybody who had ideas that were counter to his. He was afraid that people were going to steal his information. He hoarded all his new ideas and concepts, waiting for the magical day when he was going to patent all of his information and make a lot of money. He refused to collaborate on joint computer efforts because he didn't want to share his ideas until they were all patented. So Wes's great ideas sat in his own personal silo and rotted. They were never put to use. He was the city merchant refusing to share what ultimately belonged to everyone in the community.

The Buddha taught that there is no separation between our spiritual practices and our daily lives. Stealing and hoarding are like spreading dung on those you were sent to collaborate with. A stuffed silo equates to a sour soul. What you have been given needs to be spread out and shared with the world. When you stay within your own personal silo because you are afraid of lack of money, death, rejection, and shame, your soul rots like an apple at the bottom of a barrel. You need to open the storeroom of your soul, overcome your fear, and share your destiny with the world. You were sent here to collaborate with others.

Fear of Losing Control

People often refuse to collaborate because they fear losing control.[13] Linden asserts that the fear of losing control is about power. When we amass power we desire to control it. When we have ideas and concepts we feel we have to control them. If God sent us into the world with a purpose, we feel that we have a responsibility to control this destiny and its outcomes. Nothing could be further from the truth.

One thing that living in this dynamic world should teach us is that we can't control anything. We can't control the weather, we can't control diseases, and we can't control when accidents happen. On a personal level, we can't control our spouses, our children, our coworkers, or our bosses. Unfortunately, the more we try to control something, the tighter we try to grasp the person or the issue at hand. By grasping tighter we choke and suffocate those with whom we are supposed to collaborate.

Have you ever seen a small child carrying a pet hamster by the neck, its little eyes popping as it squeals? When you grip and try to control people and ideas, you suffocate them. The only way to effectively engage people and ideas is to learn to loosen your grasp and let go.

One of the greatest disciplines for adults is to be able to fall asleep. Too many people can't fall asleep because they toss and turn, worrying about people, issues, and ideas. They're grasping, clenching, and gripping their worries, trying to control them. The only way to fall asleep is to let go. You will awake in the morning with new insights and ideas. Falling asleep is the perfect exercise in learning how to let go of control. Here is an idea: set this book down and take a nap. It may be the perfect way to learn how to loosen your grip on the hamster's neck.

It's an old adage, but I find it to be so true: "Let go and let God." At some point we have to let go and allow the Creator to be the Ultimate Being. We need to do our work, bring our best to the table, dispense our information, collaborate with others, and let go.

If you are focused only on success, you will become so bound in the immediate context that you will fail to act at all. If you can be confident in your identity as someone who is sent, you can simply act, presenting your ideas to a group of people like a sacred offering, trusting along with them that the highest good will be realized.

One of the key themes that run throughout the Hindu text the Bhagavad Gita is to simply act without trying to control the results of your actions. The Gita teaches that trying to control the results is a reflection of your own ego's need for success. Wisdom is found when you stop worrying about success or failure and simply act.

> You have a right to your actions,
> But never to your actions' fruits.
> Act for the action's sake.
> And do not be attached to inaction.
>
> Self-possessed, resolute, act
> Without any thought of results,
> Open to success or failure.
> This equanimity is yoga.[14]
>
> . . . .
> Without concern for results
> Perform the necessary action;
> Surrendering all attachments,
> Accomplish life's highest good.[15]

We often want to control the results of our actions because we are not only worried about success, but also motivated by the approval of other people. The Tao Te Ching teaches that this is another trap that limits our actions.

> Care about people's approval
> And you will be their prisoner.
> Do your work, then step back.
> The only path to serenity. [16]

People tentatively hold on to their ideas, then dangle them in front of a group, ready to snatch back the idea if they don't receive the approval of the group. One of the great keys to effective collaboration is to bring as many ideas as possible to the table so that together the group can discern the best ones. Who cares if your idea is not selected? It may just have been the key insight that allowed the group to find the right concept. Besides, you can always pocket it for another time. The group process also provides wonderful ways to shape and perfect your idea.

What would happen if seven billion people were bent on control? The world would be gripped in international gridlock. Maybe that's the problem. Maybe we are trying so hard to control our own personal and national agendas that we have the globe locked up. In America, political parties have the nation in gridlock because both sides are trying to control the country. In the Middle East, religious zealots are trying to control the world through fanaticism. Other nations are choked by the control of dictators. In Mexico's border towns, thousands of people are executed by drug cartels that control police departments and citizens through terror and mayhem. We are sent into the world not to control but to collaborate. We have to let go of our desire for power and creatively interact with others.

The ability to collaborate begins with you. An inflated ego, the need to guard your turf, a silo mentality, and striving for control reflect your own personal issues. If you truly desire to fulfill the

Creator's purpose in sending you, then these issues must be confronted and moved out of the way. The ubuntu belief is that we will be fully actualized only when we empower those around us to realize their divine destinies. To empower people we are going to have to collaborate with them. By collaborating, we can fully engage our mutual destiny and together synergize for a greater purpose.

Synergy

I love being a part of a group where a creative energy has taken over and there is a sparkling buzz in the room. Ideas spin from person to person. Insights snap like firecrackers. Whiteboards fill up with ideas. The mental juice flows in such a way that the entire group is unified as a single expansive mind.

Stephen Covey, in his masterful book *The Seven Habits of Highly Effective People*, describes synergy as one of the key habits a person must develop to lead a healthy and productive life.[17] Synergy is when you see that you are part of something greater than yourself. It is when you want to pour your ideas, energy, and effort into a group process. Synergy is when you allow the ideas of others to change, inspire, and move you in new directions.

Synergy is the core essence of what it means to be in a relationship with the Ultimate Being. As people collaborate in groups, the Creator's spirit synergistically moves back and forth, creating a new dynamic.

Synergy is the process of prayer. We open ourselves up and the divine Spirit brings a flood of ideas and creativity. The Creator interacts with our thoughts, ideas, and beliefs. In the Christian New Testament there is a story about an event called Pentecost. Jesus's disciples are filled with the Holy Spirit. It's an amazing story of synergy. The Holy Spirit descends on the disciples and opens them up to a whole new world that they haven't previously seen.[18] Before the Spirit of God enters them they are frightened fishermen. Afterwards, a third dynamic enters the room. They are now greater than the sum of their individual parts. Creativity and courage flow from them. They discover new insights that they have never seen. When we collaborate with others, we find this third element; we discover an effortless flow of interacting with one another.

Taoists would use the term *wu-wei* to describe synergy. You experience wu-wei when you have stepped into the flow of the Tao in such a way that your thoughts move like an effortless stream of consciousness. As when the Holy Spirit entered the disciples, the Tao becomes that dynamic third element. As a group moves to an effortless state in which people naturally pair up and ideas ping like electrons humming around a nucleus, they have stepped into the dynamic presence of the Tao. The flow of creativity emanating from their collaboration is wu-wei.

Covey describes the key ingredients that go into creating synergy within a group.[19] It begins by valuing the differences of all those gathered at the table. As a part of this value, a safe environment must be created for everyone to openly and freely share their ideas and opinions without judgment or condemnation. Linden suggests that those at the table must go from "me" to "we." Individuals within the group need to care enough about the other people at the table to be willing to slow down the group process so that all may participate. Trust needs to build between members as they share ideas and are heard. Linden concurs with Covey that the basic habits of effective people must be constantly practiced; look for win-win solutions, seek first to understand, then to be understood. Linden encourages people to use *more pull than push* in communication. Seek to draw out from everyone their worries, fears, and concerns before you push your agenda onto others.[20]

Linden suggests group norms that should be established to foster synergy:

- Candor is essential, and there is no retribution.
- Everybody contributes and nobody dominates.
- Egos, and agency identities are left at the door.
- Differences are kept professional, not personal.
- Decisions are made at the table (no behind-the-scenes deals, no surprises).
- The group uses the seventy-percent rule . . . "Can we each get seventy percent of what we want from this proposal?"[21]

I suggest you write these norms on huge sheets of butcher paper and hang them around the meeting room. Constantly call yourself and the group back to these values.

In the church where I serve as pastor we confronted a problem for which synergy brought a solution none of us had expected. The heart of the conflict centered on where the cross was going to be placed in the sanctuary. When the sanctuary had been built some twenty years before, the cross had been attached to the front wall. The well-meaning worship committee had had a creative insight to move the cross from the front wall and suspend it over the congregation. It was going to be a great surprise, a gift they were going to give to the congregation. So one week they worked quickly to move the cross before the Sunday services. As the sanctuary doors were opened, the members of the committee were waiting proudly for their accolades. As people walked into the sanctuary, however, they were aghast to see what had happened to their cross! Murmurs of "sacrilege" were heard. Others asked, "Why weren't we consulted? Who has done this to our sanctuary?" The congregation was split between those who loved it and those who hated it. Ideological turfs were created, walls were built, silos were erected, and everyone was wrestling for control.

As I have said, "Wherever two or more are gathered in Christ's name, there's bound to be a fight."

First we created an environment of trust. The norms listed above were presented and all agreed to follow them for the benefit of the whole congregation. People began to remember that they were not enemies, but fellow members of a congregation who wanted to find a solution that met the seventy-percent rule. We began by sharing the history of who had built the cross and the original idea behind attaching the cross to the front wall. The worship committee members shared the purpose of moving the cross out over the congregation. Both sides bit their tongues and listened. The group entered a time of brainstorming, and a palpable feeling began moving through the group. It was energy, a *synergy*. It sounded so simple, but they suddenly came up with the idea of moving the cross back toward the wall, but not attached to the wall. It was a win-win solution that seventy percent of the group agreed with.

The cross was rehung in the agreed-upon space. As the lighting in the sanctuary illuminated the newly hung cross, all of the participants gave a collective gasp. What emerged from the shadows of the cross were images of two other crosses on the side walls of the front of the sanctuary. The dramatic effect captured the three crosses on Calvary. These shadows now form one of the driving images for this particular congregation. The solution would never have been discovered if the two opposing parties had not come together in the spirit of collaboration and synergy. Their solution was greater than the sum of their individual ideas.

Collaborating is hard work. As someone who is sent by the Creator, at times you will feel as though you have to sacrifice your most sacred ideas for the sake of the group. The members of this congregation had to do just that. Those who had originally designed the sanctuary had to let go of their need to control the community.

Those on the worship committee had to relinquish their desire to guard the turf of the symbols within the sanctuary. Through hard work they realized something far greater than either group alone ever would have. Within the spirit of collaboration, they realized that it's not about "you," it's about ubuntu, everyone's destiny being realized.

The But-But Game

Nothing ruins the spirit of collaboration quicker than the "But-But" game. This game is played when someone is sharing a controversial idea and instead of truly listening to what is being said, you are already forming an argument saying why it will never work. You will know you are playing the "But-But" game because the first words out of your mouth will be, "*But* that will never work . . . ," "*But* we tried that last year." If your first word is "But . . . ," you have just doused the spirit of synergy. When a group is humming with creativity and a spirit is flowing back and forth, and someone says,

"But . . . ,"

I can just feel the Creator slapping a hand to the divine forehead saying, "Dang it! Just when things were getting going!"

God does say that, I'm convinced.

When working to resolve the conflict around where to hang the cross, both parties were embroiled in the "But-But" game. "But . . . but you weren't here when the sanctuary was designed." "But . . . but your idea is sacrilegious!" "But . . . but you're not seeing the benefits of what this new idea will do!"

Breaking the "But-But" game is critical to creating a climate of trust and creativity. I helped this congregation break through the "But-But game" by placing a bowl in the center of the table. Every time someone said, "But . . . ," they had to throw in a dollar bill. It turned the conflict into a fun situation as someone would throw out a crazy idea and people would reach for their wallets. While it made everyone smile, it provided an instant metaphor for how they were breaking the spirit of synergy and collaboration.

The key is seeking ubuntu! When you are a part of a synergistic group process, you discover your identity by empowering others to discover theirs. Your creative presence allows someone else's divine destiny to come to fruition. Synergy is a holy event. When you intentionally create the spirit of ubuntu you tap into the power of the Creator working in your midst.

Collaborating on Behalf of the Galaxy

The Creator sent individuals to collaborate in groups—groups to collaborate in communities, communities to collaborate as nations, and nations to collaborate for the betterment of the globe. Will there come a time when the globe needs to collaborate for the betterment of the galaxy? I think so.

We have all been sent. What would happen? What could we create? What new age of revelation could we usher into the world if each person, group, business, church, mosque, synagogue, each place of worship, realized that we were sent to collaborate? If each group strived to embody the force of life we would become a chorus of seven billion people singing our souls out to God.

We are standing on the verge of a new creation. The Creator is presently acting in the world so that a whole new reality is shaping and forming. The Internet is unleashing a tremendous amount of creativity. As the world flattens and national boundaries become irrelevant to the ways people communicate and work together, a new spirit of collaboration has developed. You too can be a part of this great wave of creation if you realize that you are not sent solo into the world, but are sent with seven billion other people.

I believe it comes down to desire. The key to synergy and ubuntu is to "*want to*."[22] You have to want to work this way. You have to want to be this type of person. Ubuntu has to become a part of your character. It has to be the core value for effective group processes. If you or others at the table are motivated by fear, the silo mentality, turf wars, or ego needs and/or are fighting for control, then the group is gridlocked. The reason governments become gridlocked is that they lack a deep desire to collaborate. They come to the table with their arms folded and their legs crossed. Their minds are already made up. It's the same with school boards, community hearings, and homeowner associations. Behind-the-scene decisions have already been made. Community meetings are often a false pretense to appease those who are affected. There is no real collaboration, synergy is never created, and trust is destroyed. The people involved never really wanted to work together in the first place.

When people come to a group process with an angry chip on their shoulders, you have to be the one who models a different way of being. Collaboration is a challenge when you're stuck in a giant institution where you are nothing but a number or if you are part of a corporation that is focused only on the bottom line. But it's precisely collaboration and a spirit of synergy that eventually breaks through these national, corporate, or personal barriers.

Ultimately synergy and ubuntu are about love. To fulfill your divine destiny you need to embody Jesus's greatest teaching, "No one has greater love than this, to lay down one's life for one's friends."[23] Your love for others may have to be so great that you are willing to set aside what you feel are your best ideas, your greatest insights, so that the greater good might be realized. By doing so, by losing yourself, you will have found yourself. Your destiny is not a solo enterprise but a group discovery.

The seven billion people sent into the world need to come to the table and begin the process of collaboration. You are invited to join them. Get out of your silo, mow down your turf, forget about your ego, let go of control, and join the party. It's simply beautiful when all of us begin dancing to the same tune.

 ### Questions to Help You Discover and Explore Your Divine Purpose

1. Who is your favorite person on the planet to be with? Why is this so? How does that person complete your life?

2. What did Jesus mean when he said, "Whenever two or more are gathered in my name, there I am also"? When have you felt a holy presence when you were with other people?

3. If it is true that Jesus is with us when we are gathered, then why do religious people create so much conflict?

4. When have you experienced ubuntu?

5. Do you think you have a big ego? How do you know if your ego is too big?

6. What is the difference between being confident and being egotistical?

7. Who is someone that you know who is egotistical? What egotistical behaviors does that person demonstrate?

8. What turf war are you currently fighting? Why are you engaging in this battle?

9. What is the silliest example of a turf war that you have seen?

10. Who is someone that you know who has a silo mentality?

11. What gifts do you have that you are hoarding?

12. Why do people fear losing control?

13. Over whom do you wish you had more control? If you wrote "myself," what are the behaviors, thoughts, or feelings that you need to rein in?

14. Who tries to control you the most? How does it feel when that person tries to control you? Why does that person feel the need to control you?

15. Why is it hard to let go and let God? Where do you need to do this in your own life?

16. When have you experienced synergy with a group of people? What were the issues that you were working on? What created the spirit of synergy?

17. Have you ever experienced synergy with God?

18. Why is collaborating such hard work?

Steve! They're shooting! They're shooting at the high school!
Oh my God, my God!

—Phoebe Poos-Benson

Chapter Nine

The Shootings

Finally, the shootings had stopped, Columbine High School was surrounded by yellow police caution tape, and the night chill crawled down my neck, sending a shiver of despair down my spine. I asked the Jefferson County District Attorney, Dave Thomas, for permission to go into the school now that all the dead and wounded had been accounted for. He looked at me skeptically, "Why do you want to go into the school?" I knew it was an odd request, but I also knew I wanted, and needed, to go in.

"Because they're my kids, Dave—they're my kids. This happened on my watch as their pastor. I know what's in there. Their bodies are lying crumpled in the hallways and library. They're alone and I want to anoint them. It's my job. Please Dave, let me go in."

Dave hesitated, and I thought he would let me duck under the tape and slip into the hallways. For twenty years I had been coming to this school to teach classes, talk with teachers, listen to choir performances, and watch ball games. This school was an extension of my life and work. I didn't need an escort, I wasn't afraid. I just knew I needed to touch their foreheads and pray. Dave took a deep breath and looked up to the heavens as if he was seeking some divine guidance. He looked back at me and shook his head, "No, Steve. I'm sorry. I can't let you go in. This is way beyond all of us. You can go as far as the yellow caution tape, but you have to stop there."

CHAPTER NINE

I grabbed Don, a fellow pastor in the community, and walked to the school. A cop stood at the tape, and as we approached he stiffened. We told him we were pastors and just wanted to pray. The officer relaxed. He looked down and away, not wanting to meet us eye to eye. Don and I grabbed each other's hands and I started to pray. My words crumbled. I could only choke out, "God . . . help us." Little did I know we would need every ounce of divine intervention to survive the decade stretching out before us.

Everything that you have read in *Sent to Soar* is far more than techniques I have dreamt up. *Sent to Soar* is personal. My world was wracked when Eric Harris and Dylan Klebold shot and killed thirteen people and injured twenty-one before taking their own lives. Before this day, I had been a part of countless tragedies. As a volunteer firefighter I had picked up body parts one night when a man tried to beat a train at a railroad crossing. Another time my wife and I were first on the scene at an intersection on a rural road where a man and a woman ran their Harley head-on into a Nissan 4Runner. My own son had almost died several times because of a rare metabolic disorder.

But this was different.

The shootings were a watershed event in our nation's history. The whole world watched as we struggled to come together as a community. Many of the insights that we now take as accepted practice in the wake of public shootings were nonexistent. Some of the concepts you have read about in *Sent to Soar* I had been practicing for years. Others I had to learn through the scrape and battle of knitting a community back together. But everything I knew as a person and spiritual leader was challenged on April 20, 1999. The shootings were my blown radiator from chapter 4. However, there was no cute "GodStar" on the side of my head that I could push for instant divine insight. Every day presented challenges that were far beyond my capabilities. After the shootings I tore out of my theological lexicon the saying, "God never gives you more than you can handle." When people would try to mollify me with this theological toss-off I would smile and think to myself, "Bullshit." I was so far beyond being able to cope that I thought several times about leaving the ministry. Yet, I stayed and worked through the tragedy. I knew that I had come to a new level of healing and integration when I felt the impulse to write this book. I felt Jesus pointing at me to write. Lakshmi touched my forehead and said, "You know what to say." So I sat down and started writing. While I have tried to keep the stories upbeat and lighthearted, the lessons I learned, like those of your life, came out of the trenches of people's pain. I wanted to write this chapter as a way of saying that for me this book is not fluff; it's how I stitched my life back together. It's how I helped other people get back on their feet. I can only pray that it does the same for you.

April 20th, 1999

It started as a beautiful spring day. After a cold Colorado winter the air finally softened, the lawns began to green, and crocuses and tulips splashed color along sidewalks and driveways. It was 10:12 a.m. I had just checked my watch. The church staff meeting was over and I was heading to my truck. A group of pastors was gathering to swap preaching ideas at a church across town. As I walked down the hallway my cell phone rang. This was back when cell phones had just begun to enter the public market. I had convinced the church to buy them for the staff, as they would enhance our ability to communicate with each other. It was before cell phones became a vital aid to an emergency response, and kids didn't have phones stuck in their backpacks. This all changed after Columbine.

I flicked open the cover and heard my wife's panicked voice, "Steve! They're shooting! They're shooting at the high school! Oh my God, my God!" She was at a local bagel shop across from Clement Park. A carload of kids had piled into the store, screaming and crying.

As my wife yelled into the phone I thought to myself, "It's happened . . . here . . . in our community." I told her that I was going to the high school and I would keep her posted.

In that moment several thoughts raced through my head. I knew I had a choice. I had free will and could exercise it any way that suited me. I thought about going to the church office and snapping on the television to see what was being said on the news. I thought about gathering the staff and going into the sanctuary to pray. This moment was pregnant with possibilities. There was a divine bias, and I had to figure it out and choose it. Use it and choose it. This is more than a pithy saying that ended up in this book; it is a challenge that I practice daily. So I chose.

I yelled down the hall, "There's a shooting at the high school. I'm heading over." I told Dot, my secretary, "Stay by the phones, watch the news and keep me updated via the phone." Holly, the youth minister; Michael, the minister of music; and Ken, our minister of visitation, ran to the truck with me.

In the midst of any crisis, the Creator acts immediately through the processes of the contextual will described in chapter 2. It works, moves, and pushes against the challenges that impede its flow. It compels people to act and respond. At this moment Eric Harris and Dylan Klebold had unleashed a tide of evil. Concurrently a countertide of life was rising up: police officers, swat teams, sheriff's deputies, counselors, and three pastors. I was coming from the east; Don Marxhausen, a Lutheran pastor, was coming from the south;

and Rick Barger, another Lutheran pastor, was coming from the west. Each of us as an individual was compelled to act and respond as a part of the Creator's energy.

I had driven to the school thousands of times before; however, this drive was going to be different. It was now a stochastic process in which the variables were going to unfold in exponential ways. Each moment presented a new set of challenges in which a bias had to be discerned, and I had to choose.

We headed south on Platte Canyon, turned right onto Coal Mine Avenue, and raced toward Pierce Street. When I turned right onto Pierce, I saw Pam, a church member who had run from her home, standing on the corner. Her face was ashen. A police officer had stopped her from going any farther. She saw me and called out, "Oh my God, Steve! It's happened."

The policewoman stopped me. I told her that I was a pastor in the community; I knew these kids and was going to the school. She said I could go only as far as the police cars up ahead but no farther.

As you head north on Pierce, the road dips and then rises a block from the student parking lot. Police cars were nose to nose in the road, blocking access. I knew these neighborhoods and was not going to be stopped.

I knew the back way that leads directly to the main entrance of the school. There were hundreds of terrified teenagers running toward us. I turned around and looked at Holly and Michael and said, "Get out of the truck and run toward those kids!" Holly looked back at me fighting panic. She asked, "What am I supposed to do?"

"Grab the kids, get them down and away from the line of fire, get them as far away from the school as possible. You have your cell phone. We'll call each other every thirty minutes."

Michael looked at me and said, "Steve, I'm just an organist."

"Not today, you're not," I replied. "Not today."

193

My lasting memory of this moment is looking over my shoulder as I made a U-turn and watched Holly and Michael grab kids, getting them down and away from the line of fire. Holly later told me that she could hear the ricochet of bullets pinging off swing sets in Leawood Park across from where she and the kids were huddling. Holly and Michael were some of the true heroes that day.

My next thought was to wind my way over to the north entrance of the school across from Clement Park. I really had no idea what I was going to do when I got there; I just knew I was supposed to go. Clement Park surrounds the school and many of the kids use its lots to park their cars. As I drove I saw swarms of kids running blindly down the streets. I saw a member of my church, a teacher, running with them. I yelled at her, "Sally, what's happening inside?"

"We heard gunshots. I grabbed the kids and just started running."

"Keep running," I said. "Keep running deeper into the neighborhood!"

Eventually, I turned left on West Leadwood drive and was stopped by police. I pulled the truck over. Ken and I hopped out and two officers immediately stopped us. I told them that I was a pastor and knew the school, the teachers, and the kids. "I can be of help. Where is the command center?" They let me through and pointed up the road. Ken and I ran around police cars parked haphazardly along the road. Above us news helicopters were buzzing. The command center was nothing more than a series of cars parked bumper to bumper. Police officers from every surrounding district had responded. I asked one of the officers if he knew what was going on in the school. He told me that a group of black radicals had taken over the school and were holding kids hostage. "What! You've got to be kidding me." The officer turned away from me. I thought this was ludicrous. The not-so-latent racism that permeates aspects of our white suburb had raised its ugly head. I knew that what the officer told me was not possible. As people sent into situations, we are called to enter crises in a way that confronts bigotry and injustice. I was not going to stoop so low as to go along with this blatant racial bias. What was happening remained a mystery.

I am not a police officer or a military person; I had nothing on me to signify who I was. I felt shaky as I stepped up to the officer who appeared to be in charge. Once again, I repeated that I was a minister. I had worked in this community for twenty years, I knew the school, the teachers, and the parents, and I could help them. The officer held my stare. Behind me a SWAT team began piling out of a van, locking and loading automatic rifles, waiting for their orders. "Seriously! I can be of help," I repeated. What a contrast—SWAT officers armed with AR-15s, and I'm armed with the notion that I have been sent.

The lead officer looked at me and said, "Go to the library across Clement Park. I've been told there's a mass of people there and it's total chaos. Go see what you can do." I nodded in agreement and Ken and I ran toward the library.

The Columbine Community Library sits at the Northwest entrance of Clement Park. As Ken and I jogged the half mile, we ran into two freshman boys dressed in blue gym shorts and gray t-shirts, wandering around. One had a weight lifting belt draped over his shoulder. Their faces were pimpled, their hair was mussed, and they were relaxed, as if simply enjoying a stroll on a spring morning. I asked them their names and if they knew what was happening inside the school.

"We were in gym class lifting weights. Someone ran in and said there were two guys shooting and we needed to get out. So we just left the gym. We didn't know where to go, so we just started walking around the park looking for something to do."

I asked them if they were okay. They looked at me like I was a little nuts, "Of course we're okay. Why?" It felt like a Falstaff moment from Shakespeare. They were two innocent boys oblivious to the world crashing in around them. I told them to stick with us.

As we all jogged to the library, I called the group of pastors I was supposed to be meeting with. I wanted them to come and meet me in the library. The secretary answered and I explained what was happening. I asked to be transferred to the group of pastors and told her it was an emergency. I needed their help in responding to the school shootings at Columbine High School. She told me to wait.

Several minutes elapsed. As I was jogging I was thinking, "What's taking so long?"

She came back on the line and told me that the pastors had elected to stay in their meeting, "They want to prepare for their Sunday sermons."

I was dumbfounded.

I tried to hold back the sarcasm as I told the secretary, "Tell them to preach on the Good Samaritan!" and snapped the phone closed. In every moment there's a bias. The Creator acts in the midst of our circumstances. We are all given the freedom to choose how to respond. Use it and choose it—and they made their choice.

When Ken and I pulled open the library doors we entered a chaotic scene. Approximately two thousand kids attend Columbine High School. In a matter of moments the majority of them had fled the buildings, and there were approximately four thousand parents flocking toward the school, trying to find their teenagers. The television news stations were telling parents to go to either the Columbine Library or Leawood Elementary School.

As I looked around the room there were several hundred parents, some crying, others looking shocked and asking if anyone had seen their child. About a hundred kids had found their way to the library, and many more were pouring in each minute. As the numbers in the building grew, the tension was building toward panic. I looked for anyone in authority to bring order. There were no librarians to be found. There was one police officer standing in the corner. I was amazed that no one was doing anything to help calm the crowd. I called my wife, who is a trauma therapist. "Hey, I don't know where you are or what you're doing, but you need to get to the Columbine Library. It's mayhem in here and I need your help."

I then walked over to the police officer and said, "Okay . . . do you mind if I do something here? I was sent here by the officer in charge at the high school."

He gave me a puzzled look and asked, "What are you going to do?"

"I'm not quite sure yet. Just stand by me and make me look official." I took a breath, thought about looking like a fool, and stepped up on a library table. I looked over the crowd and shouted, "Hey! Hey! Can I have your attention!" The crying and screaming continued.

The police officer put his fingers to his lips and emitted a piercing whistle that got everyone's attention. "Listen to the guy on the table!" he shouted.

My knees felt a bit wobbly as I sucked up my best I-know-what-I'm-doing voice and introduced myself. I told the crowd that we needed to restore order. "We're going to figure this out," I said. "First thing. No one cries alone in here. If you're standing beside someone who's upset, hold them until we get this figured out." People started moving toward those who were visibly shaken. I then told them where I had been and what I knew up to that point.

"Let's start by trying to figure out who's in this building. Parents, if you have your kid, please go to this side of the room." I pointed over to where the students had gathered. "Teenagers! If you don't have a parent, stand over here by the officer. If there's a teacher in the room, please come and sit with these kids. Parents, if you're still looking for your child, please stand over by the librarian's desk." I was shocked as people started following my orders.

The officer looked up at me and said, "Keep it up!"

I yelled across the room at the librarian's desk. "Do you have any butcher paper? If so, let's roll out a couple of large strips and tape them up on the walls. Parents, write your name on this sheet of paper. Kids, you write your names on that sheet of paper. Here are the felt pens, let's get going."

My cell rang. It was Holly. She told me that she and Michael were fine, that they had made their way over to Leawood Elementary School, where there were hundreds of kids and parents. I told them what I was doing in the library and suggested they start doing the same. "Let's see if we can help parents and kids find each other."

Ideas about how to respond started flowing into my head. "Parents, who has a cell phone?" About ten hands went up. "Come over to the students' group and have them call their parents." Ken, our pastor of visitation, began working through the crowd, holding parents' hands and praying with those who were shaking and upset.

Another officer entered the building. It was Eric, who had been raised in my church. I had confirmed him. He was with the Aurora Police on the other side of the city. Seeing him brought a huge smile to my face.

Eric said, "I was off duty and called to offer my assistance. They sent me over here to the library. Whatever you're doing, it's working. Keep it going." Eric stood by me through the rest of the afternoon in the library. It was simply amazing to have a kid from the church, now a young adult, a police officer, standing beside me. Was it a coincidence that he was here? I believe it was a response to a divine movement sweeping over all of us.

Busloads of kids were pouring into the library. Parents, hundreds of them, began filling the library. I stood on my table and kept on shouting directions. A sense of collaboration filled the room. Parents helped other parents list their names. By this time my wife had arrived. As she walked into the room she met a trauma detective from the police department that she hadn't seen in years. Was it a coincidence that at one time they had done a tremendous amount of work together? They had an immediate rapport and began attending to the parents and kids who were weeping.

Suddenly a woman came into the library with huge carts overflowing with drinks, cookies, and pastries. "Here's some food!" she said, "It's all free. Come and get what you need." It was a local businesswoman who had spent hundreds of dollars on groceries and brought them to the library. She told me she was sitting in her office watching the news and knew she had to do something. When she heard that a large group was in the library, she had an idea. "Food! They'll need food!" She was compelled to get up out of her chair and act. It could have been just another coincidence, but I believe that something else had inspired her to join the rising tide of life. It may have felt like a small thing, but as the kids began devouring the drinks and cookies it was like manna from heaven.

From my tabletop I saw another church member, Kathy Ireland, walk into the library. "Kathy!" I yelled. "Do you have your kids?"

"I found Maggie, but I have no idea where Patrick is!"

"We'll find him, Kathy. I'm sure he's okay. He could be over at Leawood Elementary. There's another huge group there."

At this point none of us knew that Patrick had been shot twice in the head and once in the foot in the school library. Patrick was the young man who climbed out of the library window and fell into the arms of the Lakewood SWAT team. The SWAT officers had climbed on top of a Loomis armored truck they had pressed into duty. It was a television clip that ran thousands of times over the ensuing years.

As my wife began working with the police detective, names of the wounded kids were being reported. They gave me the names, and I asked these parents to join the detective and the therapist in the adjacent office. A sudden hush filled the room as parents knew they were being singled out for a reason. It couldn't be good news. When a wail came from one of the offices, parents outside silently began weeping, as they knew what it meant. We had to get these parents to the hospital. I asked for volunteers; immediately strangers volunteered to drive parents to the hospitals where their children were being treated.

The library was filling to capacity. The police sealed off the building, prohibiting any more adults from entering. They were, however, allowing all teenagers to enter. As the teenagers were shepherded in we added their names to the list, gave them something to eat, and kept trying to match names with parents.

Holly called me from Leawood Elementary, "We're thinking that you have kids over there and we have their parents over here. How can we connect them up?"

"Let me read you the names of the kids that we have." I began listing the names off the butcher paper.

"I can't hear you!" Holly yelled into the phone. "There's too much noise!"

As I stood on the tabletop, we brainstormed a solution.

Outside the library every television station from the city had set up cameras. I took the list and told the reporters what was happening in the library and that we needed their help. They switched on their cameras and I read the name of each teenager we had on our list.

The group over at Leawood Elementary watched the news station and was able to match parents with kids.

Eric told me that the main incident center was being moved to Leawood Elementary School. "We need to move all of these kids and parents two miles East." Ken, Eric, and I were brainstorming different ideas for moving everyone—using parents to drive kids, and so on—when suddenly several school buses pulled up. What a relief! We loaded the kids on the buses and told the parents to drive or walk. My wife was still working with the detective; I told her that I was walking to Leawood Elementary and that we would meet up later. We hugged each other and left.

As I walked, I called Dot back at the church. She said she was being bombarded with phone calls. We scheduled a community worship service for that evening. My mind was reeling with the events of the day. Had this really happened to us? One thought kept on ringing in my brain: "You will be a minister to my people." I fought back the tears and just walked on.

At Leawood Elementary there was a tearful reunion as Holly, Michael, Ken, and I hugged each other. I met other church members and former staff members who had all gathered to support one another. The word spread that Patrick Ireland had been shot and was in critical condition. We were told that Kathy and John, his parents, were already at the hospital. We all looked at one another, grief-stricken. One of the Irelands' friends crumpled to the ground. We helped her up and just held one another for a few moments.

I have seen many things in my years as a pastor; none of them can compare to the relief of watching parents reuniting with their teenagers that day. However, I have also seen nothing emptier than watching the numbers of parents dwindle down, those remaining filled with a sick sense of dread. I offered my continued assistance, but the sheriff told me that the building was being closed and our help was no longer needed.

As the April sun began to set, District Attorney Dave Thomas started to walk to the police command center. Pastor Don and I walked with him. We were all beyond exhausted as the adrenalin of the day began to wane. It was then that I asked Dave if Don and I could go into the building. I had anointed hundreds of people who were dying or dead, as this is a significant rite of our faith. Dave thought about it and shook his head, no. Pastor Don and I ended the exhausting day on the bluff overlooking the school, praying and weeping.

The Second Day

The twenty-first of April was just as chaotic as the twentieth. National networks set up huge vans, generators, lights, and radio towers. Thousands of people from across the city began pouring into Clement Park. Hundreds lined up to walk to the top of Rebel Hill, the bluff above the school. The cars belonging to some of the murdered kids were still parked in Clement Park. They were now adorned with roses, cards, candles, and bears. Teenagers walked about dazed and weeping. I had called all the pastors I knew and asked them to come to the park to be with people. As far as I know, only one responded. Use it and choose it. Everybody has to choose how they are going to respond in the midst of a crisis. In the years since the shootings I have talked with hundreds of religious leaders, encouraging them to always take the risk and go where people are hurting.

My cell phone rang. The voice on the other end had the tone of an old friend. "Steve . . . "

"Yes . . . "

"This is Stone Phillips's secretary from *Dateline*."

I held the phone at arm's distance, looking at it like it might bite my ear. "Hmm, yeah . . . really? How can I help you?"

"Well Steve, we were told that you played a big part in yesterday's tragedy and we want you on our show tomorrow."

"You're kidding."

"No, I'm serious. We want you on *Dateline*."

I hate to admit it, but my ego began to swell. Just think, I was going to be on network news. I was going to be recognized for the work that I did. The section I wrote on ego in chapter 8 is not just theory. It's something that I know personally and wrestle with daily. There is no greater impediment to the work of the Creator than one's own ego. Mine was just getting ready to stand in the way.

"However, Steve, we don't want you to come alone."

I hesitated. "You don't?"

"No, we want you to bring John and Kathy Ireland with you."

I was confused. How had they figured out that I was the Irelands' pastor? I responded to Mr. Phillips's secretary, "So, you want me to contact the Irelands and invite them to come on *Dateline*? Is that right?"

"Yes, we were hoping that since you're their pastor they might trust you more than us and would then agree to join you on the show."

I don't always say or do the right thing. I don't always "use it and choose it" appropriately. This time however, I think I got it right. "No, thank you."

"What? You don't want to come on *Dateline*?"

"No. No, thank you."

"Well Steve, you're missing quite the opportunity to share your story with the nation. You're going to be approached by several other networks. All I ask is that you reconsider and give me a call first."

"I'm honored that you would consider me for your show. But no, thank you. Don't worry, I won't speak to the other networks, and please don't call me again." As I closed my phone I had this overwhelming desire to take a shower.

That afternoon I drove to St. Anthony Hospital, where Patrick Ireland had been rushed after he fell from the window. I wanted to see John and Kathy, not to tell them about *Dateline*'s offer, but to regain a sense of balance and purpose.

The hospital was packed with kids sitting in vigil outside Patrick's room. For the next several days I would come to sit with the family. Later that week, when I visited Pat his head was wrapped in cotton gauze and bandages. His face and eyes were swollen. Language was difficult for him. He looked at us and said, "Forgive them, please forgive them." Kathy said, "Why should I forgive them?" Patrick responded,

"Because they didn't know what they were doing."

I was silent. This young man had been shot in the head twice. Bullet fragments were embedded in his skull. His foot was torn apart. Two crazed teenagers had murdered his friends and tried to do the same to him. Yet he spoke the most profound words I had ever heard.

Over the next year, television networks around the nation asked for interviews. Eventually I agreed to be part of a reflection piece sponsored by *20/20*. It was less than a stellar experience. I can't remember the interviewer from *20/20*; all I remember is that it was intellectual swordplay. He wanted me to reveal information that I felt was confidential, and I refused to budge. He had heard a sermon that I had preached on forgiveness the month before. He asked me on tape if it was really any of my business to challenge people to forgive after a massacre like the Columbine shootings. Who was I to preach on forgiveness? he asked.

I thought of Patrick Ireland now in Craig Rehab hospital. I looked the interviewer in the face and said, "If it's none of my business to preach about forgiveness, then I have no business being in this business." I was told that statement never made the piece. I will never know. I never watched the show.

Putting It All Together

The shootings at Columbine challenged me to my core. While the day of the shootings was filled with adrenaline, the years that followed were filled with the slow pain of trying to make sense of it all. Part of my healing was trying to understand how it happened and how to move forward. I am far from having all of the answers; this book is simply what I have discerned to date.

As I worked though my own emotional issues in the year after the shooting, I had to ask and answer the question, "How could two eighteen-year-old boys plan and hope to carry out the execution of hundreds of their fellow classmates and teachers?" It was Patrick Ireland's charge to forgive them that drove my research. While volumes have been written about Eric and Dylan since the shootings, I simply conclude that they chose to embody an evil force; a force of e-v-i-l that ran counter to the force of l-i-v-e. Day by day, bit by bit, they slowly stepped down a slippery slope that led to destruction. I came to know the family of one of the shooters personally; I have church members who are best friends of the other. I can tell you they are wonderful people no different from you or me. They faced the challenge of raising teenagers. As someone who has raised three teenagers myself, I identify with their pain. Many parents of troubled teenagers could tell you, and have told me, "It could have been my kid." Somewhere, Eric's and Dylan's lives went awry. I don't blame their parents or their families; I blame Eric and Dylan and hold them accountable.

I have also forgiven them.

I contend that the spark of the Ultimate Being was not completely snuffed out in their lives. I believe that up until the day of the shootings, the divine spirit within them was working, moving, pushing, trying to realign their lives. The moment they pulled the trigger, I believe there was a deep sigh of divine grief.

As I worked to understand their actions, I came to a clear sense that they were not sent into the world as a scourge. It was not the initial intention for their lives to end in a shooting massacre. It was not a reflection of their dharma; the Tao did not lead them to this. No, Eric and Dylan chose; they chose to do this evil. They used their free will for destructive ends. It was an ugly hairball. As I sat down to write *Sent to Soar* I knew that the chapter on evil was a central aspect of the book. I couldn't write about a divine purpose for life without addressing why some people choose evil.

However, I also agree with Patrick's statement, "They didn't know what they were doing." The words echo Jesus's words on the cross, "Father, forgive them; for they do not know what they are doing."[1] It's not that Patrick or Jesus did not want to hold the perpetrators accountable. Instead, it's a profound insight that keeps us from playing God.

While Eric and Dylan used their free will to choose this violence, were there extenuating circumstances that none of us were aware of? Were their psyches affected by a mental illness that made them vulnerable to violent behavior? Can an eighteen-year-old completely understand the devastation that he is going to wreak? No, I don't think so. Patrick's insight that the two teenagers did not know what they were doing encourages me to hold on to their humanity. By holding on to their humanity, I preserve my own. To be honest, half the time I don't understand my own motivations. How could I ever presume to fully understand someone else's? I forgave them because I know that I need to be forgiven. In the wake of my own mistakes and errors I also stand in need of mercy. They were human, I'm human, and you are human. At times, we are messy creations. We were created in the image of the Ultimate Being, yet somehow, there must be a wart on the divine chin, because we have that blemish. We are perfect and flawed, whole but broken, divine yet human. We were sent into the world to unleash divine potential. Can it be that the greatest potential is to forgive and be forgiven? We have the potential to forgive someone else primarily to practice the most difficult aspect of life, to forgive oneself. It is potential that I hope to realize.

In the wake of the shootings there was no time to look for blame; people's lives were devastated and we needed to respond. In an effort to heal the community many action groups were created. From the moment they were convened conflict arose. The tragedy seemed to push on every raw wound in Littleton. We were split theologically. Evangelical Christians poured into the community wanting to use this as an opportunity to convert people to Jesus. There was a nationally televised memorial service in which Billy Graham Jr. preached that all we needed to do was accept Jesus. I felt angry and nauseated watching it on the television. I wondered if Jesus liked being used as a pat answer to people's suffering. Those of us on the other end of the theological spectrum wanted to use the tragedy to heal and serve the traumatized. My understanding of collaboration came from working in the trenches trying to empower schools to collaborate with churches, churches with businesses, businesses with political officials, and political officials with police and sheriff's departments. I felt we would have had more success if we had tried to walk on water.

The tragedy forced us to face the shadow side of our community. One of the most frustrating things that people said was, "Shootings like this aren't supposed to happen here!" I would respond in exasperation,

"Where are they supposed to happen?"

The summer after the shootings my thirteen-year-old nephew from the inner city of Miami came to visit us. When he told his friends that he was going to Littleton they warned him, "Dude, are you sure it's safe to go?"

As suburbanites we tacitly believe that if we move deep into our enclaves away from the inner city, then we will be free from inner-city issues. The Columbine shootings destroyed that naïveté. We had to ponder the effect of suburban homes where neighbors are strangers even though they live ten feet apart. What is the impact where a mall substitutes for a city center? In Jefferson County, Colorado, we have one of the highest teen suicide rates in the country. The shootings removed the boundaries between inner-city problems and suburban problems, and instead we came to see our challenges as human problems, challenges that we all have to face. From the shadows we found light through building bridges of reconciliation.

I clearly learned that collaboration begins with "want to." If you want to collaborate, you will find a way to set aside your agenda and work together. Otherwise, your ego and fear block the path at every juncture. Lori, a colleague of mine who responded on the day of the shootings, was instrumental in creating a community group that worked to heal the rifts. As a part of this effort, I saw people build silos, guard their turf, puff up their egos, and try to control outcomes. It was also during this time that I discovered a true attitude of ubuntu. People from all different faith backgrounds collaborated for the good of the community. It can be done. People from different traditions can work together to fulfill a greater purpose; we can do something glorious on behalf the Creator who sent us.

The shootings taught me to understand suffering. As a pastor, I have sat with families as they tried to make sense of the murder of a loved one. But somehow, the suffering in the wake of the Columbine shootings was different. In part, it was because we as a nation were just learning about domestic terrorism. The massacre happened on the one-year anniversary of the Oklahoma City bombing. This type of terror was not a part of the American lexicon, especially not the lexicon of suffering. The Columbine shootings were a global watershed that changed our view of what could happen in schools, hospitals, business, movie theaters, and churches. We had to learn that terrorism strikes deep into the cords of dysfunction within institutions. As a result of Columbine, my congregation experienced seven years of turmoil as we had disagreements that led to church fights, conflicts, splits, and financial hardship. There has since been a tremendous amount of research about the need to work with individuals and organizations after an act of domestic terrorism. Unfortunately, it was the Columbine shootings that shook the nation awake and told us we need to prepare for such trauma and how to respond when it comes crashing into our lives. What we learned in Littleton was that no one has to suffer alone.

At Columbine United Church, and in congregations, synagogues, temples, and mosques across the city, we worked to create solid relationships through small groups, special counseling centers, and community projects. We discovered that the Creator works through people when they reach out to others in the midst of suffering. Trauma is a spooky thing. It reaches out and grabs your soul years after an event. You think you've gotten over it, and then you listen to a newscast and suddenly your eyes well with tears. It's a mystery to me how the memory of a distant tragedy can feel as close as yesterday, and yet we have to hunt for a recollection of love that has recently been bestowed upon us. This is why it has taken thousands and thousands of people engaged in l-i-v-e to offset the e-v-i-l brought by two teenage boys.

As with all trauma, I learned in this instance, too, that eventually you heal, but this doesn't mean you get over it. Instead, you get through it. However, you get through it, not alone, but always with someone else. I realized that being sent into the world ultimately means being sent to hold someone who is suffering.

The Push

I have worked for thirteen years to fulfill Patrick's charge to forgive them. I learned that it was one thing to forgive Eric and Dylan. It's a completely different challenge to forgive yourself and others in the wake of a tragedy like the shootings at Columbine High School. Forgiveness is not something you do once, but a life-long habit, a daily occurrence. In the year after the shootings I kept Patrick's admonition ever before me when I thought of Eric and Dylan. In the years since, I have learned that "We must forgive them" begins with the person in the mirror and extends to everyone you encounter. It is ultimately why we have all been sent.

I knew that I had come to a different state of integration when I felt a compulsion, a push, a command even, to take what I had learned in the years since the shootings and bring it to a broader audience. I have spoken to churches, communities, and interfaith groups, but when Lakshmi visited me through the vision I described earlier in "My Story," I knew I needed to go public, get untied from my inhibitions, and put it in writing. It started with a cell phone call in a hallway; it has concluded with what you now hold in your hands.

Questions to Help You Discover and Explore Your Divine Purpose

1. As of the writing of this book, there have been over 131 school shootings. Which one has touched you the most?

2. How do you reconcile the paradox between young people who cause violence and the good families that raised them? Are the families to blame? If so, how?

3. What was the most dangerous thing that you did as a teenager? How were your actions a reflection of your family?

4. If you have raised teenagers, what was the greatest challenge that you faced with them? What were you afraid that they would do?

5. In your opinion, what is the cause of school shootings? How do you think they should be stopped?

6. What role do you play in bringing these shootings to an end? How is that role a part of the reason you were sent?

Until one is committed, there is hesitancy, the chance to draw back, always ineffectiveness. . . . There is one elementary truth the ignorance of which kills countless ideas and splendid plans: that the moment one definitely commits oneself, the providence moves too. A whole stream of events issues from the decision, raising in one's favor all manner of unforeseen incidents, meetings and material assistance, which no man could have dreamt would have come his way. I learned a deep respect for one of Goethe's couplets: "Whatever you can do or dream you can, begin it. / Boldness has genius, power and magic in it!"

—William Hutchison Murray

Chapter Ten

Sent to Soar!

Engage—you have to engage; like locking in the hubs of a four-wheel-drive truck or strapping on a chute and jumping out of a plane, you have to stop dreaming and actually do it. You were not sent into this world to live a mundane, day-to-day existence. You were sent to soar! You were sent to collaborate with billions of other people to alleviate suffering, overcome evil, and create something marvelous for God. The question becomes: When will you commit to pursue your purpose? What will it take for you to take these final steps and launch into the life that the Creator dreamt for you? You have to bring clarity to your decision, align the energy of your life, and hear a cosmic resounding Yes! to your future.

Clarity

Your first step is clarity. It's time to go beyond a fuzzy idea of what you think your destiny is; you have to state it. Right now . . . write it out. Don't be timid, don't hold back, just write what your heart is telling you. If you are sent to be a carpenter, then get clear with this. If the Creator sent you to be a parent, then embrace this mission. If you were sent to be a lawyer, then commit to this purpose in your heart. If wandering, wondering, and contemplating life was the divine dream for your life, then dive into this journey with passion.

Take a minute and write it out. Finish the sentence, "The Creator sent me into the world to . . . "

When you clarify your divine purpose you feel a deep sense of celebration, awe, and affirmation—your life is on the right track. When you bring clarity to your destiny what you are really saying is, "Yes! Yes, I'm claiming it! Yes, I'm doing what I was preknown for! Yes! I'll go forward with my destiny! Yes!"

When you say Yes! another entity echoes your affirmation. Your Yes! is echoed by God's Yes! The Christian New Testament describes it like this:

> God's yes and our yes together [are] gloriously evident. God affirms us, making us a sure thing in Christ, putting his Yes within us. By his Spirit he has stamped us with his eternal pledge—a sure beginning of what he is destined to complete.[1]

The Creator responds to your Yes! with a divine promise: "Yes, I will be with you! Yes, I will open doors for you! Yes, I will bring you people, ideas, resources, and finances. Yes! Yes! Yes!"

Look at the epigraph at the beginning of the chapter. William Hutchison Murray describes the effect of God's yes in our lives. Murray declares that when we commit, "then providence moves, too." When we commit ourselves, we bring clarity to our destiny; then a cosmic floodgate of abundance swings open. We are bombarded with ideas and concepts. I believe in the saying, "When you make a decision, the whole universe conspires to make it happen."[2] People suddenly appear in your life in what appear to be bizarre coincidences. But they are not coincidences at all; it's the universe affirming and empowering your commitment. Often total strangers have just the right piece of information that you need at just the right time. When you walk into a bookstore, book titles jump out at you, magazines find their way into your hands. True, you have to be working, researching, writing, and planning, but when you commit and go public with your destiny, the Creator becomes active in amazing ways. The divine force that was content to let you sit and fritter away your time and talents is now active, moving, and working with you to fulfill your purpose.

Going Public

Once you have committed yourself, the next step is going public with your Yes! Many people make the mistake of saying yes in their souls, but saying nothing with their mouths. When you give voice to your commitment, when you tell others how you are going to change your life, the drive within you begins to deepen. Your dreams are out of the closet; you have taken the step to publically claim the new identity toward which you are working.

When you go public two things happen. First, there are those who criticize and belittle you. Your vision threatens them because either they have let go of their own dreams, or your new plans directly affect them. This is one reason you have to develop a rhino hide as you embark on this journey. Your skin has to become so thick that their negativity will not deter your dreams and desires.

Since going public can be a risk, I want you to think about *whom* you want to go public with. Who will be supportive of your dreams? I encourage you to name at least five people. Beside each name describe what role you hope they will play in your process. Do you want them to give you advice? Pray for you? Share their experience with you? Give you blessing and encouragement? Building a positive support network around yourself before you announce your dreams creates a buffer against those who are negative and resentful.

The second aspect of going public is that you draw other like-minded people to yourself. You become a magnet. When people hear that you are embarking on a new journey, it encourages them to share what they are trying to do with their lives. Energy begets energy. Creativity fuels the creativity in others. Those who take risks and go out on a limb encourage others to do the same. Together you create a synergy of potential. You can share with each other your hopes and desires. You can begin collaborating on the new projects that you are hoping to create and develop.

When you go public your mentor appears. There's an old adage, "When the student is ready, a teacher appears." When you commit yourself, it doesn't take long for you to realize that you have no idea how to start your journey. That's when a teacher appears who guides you. As the internal magnet of your desires begins humming, it draws you to someone who has been down the same path before. Sometimes you must intentionally seek a teacher. You have to talk with others who are pursuing the same passions. At other times, the teacher just magically appears.

Ron's life had come to a crisis point. He was frustrated with his job, he wanted to switch directions, and he was desperately unhappy, but he didn't quite know what to do. When he made the commitment to do whatever it took to change his life and he shared his dreams with those closest to him, things began to change. A network started developing; people began connecting Ron to other people who were trying to do the same. Now, it took a lot of work on Ron's part. He had to spend lunch breaks, evenings, and weekends creating this network.

Ron made lists, trying to discern his divine convergence. While he was in the midst of this process, people told him that he needed to meet Ann, a professional life coach. They had coffee and Ron shared where he was in the process of changing his life. Ann invited him to join six other people that she was mentoring in the same process. Ron suddenly had a positive community around him. Ann's experience and expertise in helping people make life transitions made her an insightful mentor. Ann helped Ron to bring focus to the direction he needed to take with his life and to discern where he was still hooked to issues from his past.

Ann brought to the surface a critical insight for Ron: the more you bring clarity to your purpose, go public with your desire, and deepen your commitment, the more you begin to realize what keeps you bound to your past.

Getting Untied

In the Christian New Testament, Jesus fulfills his destiny as he rides into Jerusalem on a colt. While he is outside Jerusalem, he tells his disciples where they can find the colt. Jesus tells them, "If anyone asks you, 'why are you untying it?' just say this, 'The Lord needs it.'"[3] I have always loved this story because it's a symbol for our need to get untied from certain relationships, jobs, or ideas so that our divine dream can be realized.

Julie was a woman who had a deep sense that the Creator was calling her to leave her suffocating marriage. Julie's gifts were tied up like that colt. She had one reason after another for not using her gifts and pursuing her destiny—four little children, her job as an accountant, her clients, and a mortgage. Most important, she had sworn to be faithful to her marriage vows. Even though Julie's soul was drying up like a sponge, she refused to make any move to free her life.

Julie had rope after rope tied to her soul. But what really had Julie tied up was the sense that she wasn't worthy. She could not come to terms with the notion that the Creator would call and free her from her suffocating marriage so that she could live, celebrate life, and fulfill her destiny.

Finally, the internal tension became too great and she made a commitment to leave her marriage. She went public by sharing her plans with me. I told her that fulfilling a destiny sometimes takes drastic and dramatic moves. For Julie it might take filing for divorce. I told Julie that while I'm very serious about marriage, I also don't believe the Creator intended marriage to be a prison sentence. Good, healthy marriages bring life and blessing. But if a marriage is stifling, oppressive, or violent, then we should leave that relationship so that we can experience the joy of living our purpose.

Other things besides marriages and jobs can tie us up. Your addiction to alcohol, drugs, sex, or work may have you tethered to a post. For example, Jack is an amazing salesman. When you are around Jack you can tell that God sent him to be in sales. Jack's warm, affable personality draws clients and businesses like moths to a lightbulb, but he is also an alcoholic. Repeatedly Jack would wake up from a three-day binge wondering where he was and what had happened to him. As the addiction took over Jack's life it destroyed his ability to sell. People could sense that something was wrong with him, and they distanced themselves from him and his business. Jack's wife left him and his adult children wanted nothing to do with him. His purpose was being drowned one shot glass at a time. Jack's addiction was robbing him of the plans and blessings the Creator intended for him.

One morning Jack woke up yet again from a long binge and realized he didn't have to live that way. Jack knew that God had intended him for something else. On Christmas Eve, as Jack was driving by a church, he felt as if a divine hand was steering his car into the parking lot. A service had just started and Jack slunk in and took a seat in the back of the sanctuary. As the service continued and Jack sang the old familiar carols, he became aware that he needed to go in a new direction. Jack realized that he had a dream to fulfill, and he summoned the courage to reach out and get help. As Hallmark as this story may seem, it's true. Jack came to see me after that Christmas Eve service, and we set an appointment to talk. It was a long battle, but eventually Jack was able to untie himself from his addiction, and he is now back using his gifts to fulfill the Creator's purpose for his life.

Sometimes we're tied to memories and feelings of regret. Jerry was very bitter about his relationship with his emotionally distant father. Not once in his entire life had Jerry heard his father say, "I love you." He had gone to great lengths to try to earn his father's love, but the words of blessing never crossed his father's lips. Even after Jerry's father had been dead for years, the bitterness that Jerry felt was like a dried peach pit in his gut. It kept him from freely experiencing love with his spouse and his children. As his father had kept him at an emotional arm's length, so did Jerry with the people around him. He could not bring forth the love and joy that were intended for his life.

Jerry had to engage the process of forgiveness so that he could let go of his father's lack of love and move on with his life. Forgiving was not easy. It took time, insight, patience, and counseling. But once fully realized, forgiveness allowed Jerry to let go of his father and begin to experience the joy and love of his present relationships.

Any number of things can tie up a person. I wonder what you find yourself tied to. Are you dying inside because you are not bringing forth that which is within you? As you dress in the morning are you putting on clothes that reflect your destiny, or are you putting on a costume that conceals who you were intended to be? There is only one person who can undo the knots that have you tethered—you!

Overcoming the Negative

The frustrating part of engaging your divine destiny is that while you become excited and passionate, others will think you are throwing your life away. When you commit yourself, engage, go public, bring clarity, and intentionally untie yourself from your tethers, you will be bombarded with negativity. People will often think you are being foolish. They will say you're too old, too young, you don't have the right gifts, or that they need you too much. These negative people are often the ones who benefit the most when you stay stuck in your life. If you change your life, they will have to change theirs. They too will have to discern what their own lives are all about. For some people that prospect is too threatening, so they do everything they can to tighten the ropes around your soul. But instead of holding you down, their negativity can positively affirm that you are on the right track. I take my insight from Jesus, who faced nothing but opposition from those around him.

When Jesus preached his first sermon in Nazareth, telling his friends and family why God had sent him, they were indignant and enraged. They were so angry they picked him up and tried to throw him off a cliff.[4] Every time Jesus said, "The Father and I are one," people tried to stone him. They couldn't stand the fact that he had the audacity to claim this unique oneness with God. The people hated that he knew why he was sent into the world and had the courage to fulfill that purpose! Jesus warned that you might experience persecution from people around you. But instead of this negativity discouraging you, it should propel you into your future. Jesus said,

> Count yourselves blessed every time people put you down or throw you out or speak lies about you to discredit me. What it means is that the truth is too close for comfort and they are uncomfortable. You can be glad when that happens—give a cheer, even!—for though

they don't like it *I* do! And all heaven applauds. And know that you are in good company. My prophets and witnesses have always gotten into this kind of trouble.[5]

When you go public with the Creator's dream for your life and people belittle you, discount you, or think you're just plain nuts, it's time to rejoice! As Jesus said, their negativity affirms that you have found the truth about your life.

Like an addict that often has to leave behind friends and associates who enable and encourage the addiction, you may need to change your relationships. It's bad enough that you bombard your brain with negative self-talk; it's even worse when people around you intentionally suffocate divine desires.

It usually starts with childhood. Children are naturally curious about their lives and their futures. Children love to explore what they want to be when they grow up. Unfortunately, parents, family members, and teachers can dam spirits and stifle aspirations. I call this "spiritual abuse." Just as there are people who are physically, emotionally, and verbally abusive, so are there those who are spiritually abusive. These negative people knock about people's souls with sacred scriptures. The Bible, the Koran, the Bhagavad Gita, and the Torah are used as spiritual baseball bats. These spiritually abusive people are often those who are held up as holy people: pastors, priests, imams, and rabbis. They leave memories like tapes that play an unending chorus of degradation and haunt people throughout their lives.

I am constantly amazed when I hear great artists, musicians, and engineers tell stories about their childhood when parents, a teacher, a coach, or a pastor told them they couldn't sing, they couldn't paint, they would never amount to anything. These people then spent years and years working to overcome this negativity to achieve the full potential that the Creator gave them.

I work with an amazing artist and musician, Mitch. His parents never once praised him, shared with him how much they loved him, or voiced their pride in his skills. Now as an adult Mitch tells me that with every new piece of music he writes and performs, he's looking in some way for his parents' praise. He feels a deep spiritual ache because his parents never blessed his gifts.

How many parents, teachers, pastors, and priests have stifled God's destiny for children and teenagers? If you are someone in one of these roles, then part of your sacred purpose is to empower the dreams and imaginations of children. Tell them repeatedly that they are sacred, special—a great gift to the world!

Adults coming out of their spiritual closet face the same challenge when they confront other adults who are threatened. When parents scoff at your spiritual dreams, it hurts whether you're fifteen or fifty-five. When your spouse scoffs at your aspirations and tells you that there is no way you can fulfill these desires, it feels like a hammer rapping the knuckles of your soul.

Leanne had a strong desire to go back to school and become a nurse. She knew that this is what God sent her to do; but Mike, her husband, refused to participate in her dreams. He felt that Leanne was too old to go back to school and that it would put them at risk financially. So Leanne kept putting off her dreams of nursing. The longer she put off her desire, the more her soul felt suffocated. Jesus's teaching was coming true: "If you do not bring forth what is within you, what you do not bring forth will destroy you."[6] When Leanne and Mike talked to me I challenged them to dream and risk together so that both of them could fulfill the Creator's desires for their lives.

Like old drinking buddies that can keep an alcoholic stuck in addiction, so friends and families can keep you stuck in your life.

You can be tied to their opinions as the colt was tied in Jesus's story. However, there comes a time when, in order to pursue your sacred dreams, you must untie yourself or cut yourself free. People may feel you're foolish or crazy or have lost your mind; really, what you have done is found your soul. You must let go of the negativity from your childhood. Say No! to the negative messages that echo in your brain. Don't let spiritually abusive people discourage or dampen your soul's desire. Keep on pushing, opening your life so that you can engage in what you were sent to do.

Alignment

When I was a teenager I had an old pickup that would constantly go out of alignment. It would be fine until I hit sixty miles an hour. Then the steering wheel would chatter like the teeth of a naked man in a snowstorm. I would have to constantly slow down to keep myself on the road. It's the same with your life; if you don't have all aspects of your being aligned with your purpose, you will have to take it slow or else wobble along. To gain momentum and start accelerating into your destiny, you have to align your daily schedule toward these ultimate goals.

Stephen Covey said it best: our lives are filled with the thick of thin things. We are endlessly distracted with e-mail, snail mail, text messages, voice mail, wandering around the Internet, wandering around in our lives like a drunk searching for his car after he leaves the bar. The Creator's dream is unleashed only when you remove the thin things from your life and focus on the great reason you were sent.

You have to reorder your priorities. I highly recommend a book like Covey's if you need to learn the process of setting first things first.[7] Covey likens time management to filling a jar with rocks. Most people fill the jar of their schedule with sand and pebbles. These represent the small distractions of life. Then with the little amount of space left, people put in the big rocks of their major commitments. But the jar is so filled with the little distractions there is no room for the priorities that would enable them to fulfill their destiny.

Your rock, your priority, your first commitment around which you need to schedule everything else is your divine destiny. You must accept this and agree to collaborate with the Creator to bring it to fruition. Every week ask yourself, "What steps do I need to take this week to unleash my purpose?" These steps are your "first things" that you prioritize in your schedule. If you are a parent of young children, setting aside even a little bit of time may be quite challenging. If you are in the midst of a busy career, adding something new to your schedule can seem daunting. But all it takes is one significant step a day. If you can schedule that one step each day over a period of months or years, you will have taken major leaps toward accomplishing the purpose for which you were sent.

Alignment has to do with every part of your life. As your commitment deepens, it becomes very apparent which aspects of your life are propelling the divine dream and which are limiting it. Alignment is the intentional process through which you evaluate your friends, relationships, hobbies, and habits. If some part of your life is throwing you off track, remove it. If a hobby consumes an undue amount of time, it needs to be postponed. If a negative person demands attention, that person needs to be quieted. People may tell you that you are being rude, distant, uncaring, or too intense. Again, this criticism lets you know you are on the right course. When these distractions are removed and your life becomes aligned with your purpose, momentum builds each day and becomes exponential. Once the wobble is removed, your life gets traction as you drive yourself into your future.

The Plateau

While there is a great deal of excitement around engaging your destiny, there will also be times when the energy is gone. Instead of going forward, you will feel as if you are wandering in a wasteland. Your divine purpose will begin to feel stagnant, like scum on a pond. Instead of collaborating, you will feel yourself at loggerheads, not only with groups you are working with, but even with the Creator. The dynamic energy that once got you out of bed and filled you with desire is now an empty bucket. You are now unsure what you're supposed to be doing. You doubt your divine purpose and you are wondering if God ever sent you in the first place. If this describes you, welcome to the spiritual plateau.

While it can feel like drudgery, the plateau is an important part of engaging your divine purpose. It is a sign of maturity. You wouldn't be experiencing this long stretch if you had not done some serious climbing. So if you find yourself on a plateau, accept it as a positive place to be. It's not that you are lost or distanced from the Creator; it's just that you need to pause on your path.

You may be on a plateau because your purpose is evolving. Remember the analogy of the archer. You were shot into the creation, toward a grand destination. Being on the plateau prepares you for the next step in the journey. The plateau helps you realize that you may need to completely change your flight path.

If you feel as though you are on a plateau because you are being sent in a different direction, I invite you to return to the five questions in chapter 5. What are your passions, joys, fears, angers, and gifts? Spend time working on your divine convergence. By working through these questions, you may find that you need to let go of your past accomplishments and head down a new path. This is what happened to the apostle Paul in the Christian New Testament.

Paul was convinced he needed to go to the city of Troas, but every time he tried to head that direction he encountered one impediment after another.[8] Eventually, he realized that God was blocking his way. Instead of fighting it, Paul sat and waited. Eventually, a dream led him to Macedonia. Paul was being sent in a completely different direction. Because he listened, Paul was able to spread the Gospel throughout the Roman Empire. Is the Creator blocking your way? Are you on the plateau because you need to see something new about your life and your divine destiny? If so, then use this plateau to discover and explore new directions.

Time spent on the spiritual plateau matures your soul. Use the space of the plateau to return to the spiritual disciplines of meditation, reflection, and writing. Read from the great spiritual masters in history. Read outside the religion that you profess. Turn to such books as the Tao Te Ching, and the Bahagavad Gita, or to the Sufi poets Rumi and Hafiz. Read the Jewish scriptures, the Christian New Testament, or the Koran. Explore the Yoga Sutras of Patanjali, one of the oldest spiritual masters in history. Many people never read other sacred texts because they are afraid those texts contain heresy. Nothing could be further from the truth! Each of these sacred texts and authors expands your understanding of what it means to be a child of the Creator. In the midst of the plateau they guide you across your spiritual wasteland.

However, people often tell me that while on the plateau they don't feel like praying or reading the scriptures. I tell them, "So don't!" Don't force what doesn't feel right, but return to that which brings you joy. Are you doing those things that open your heart? Are you intentionally filling your life with meaning? The plateau can be a time to relax, breathe, and rediscover a sense of rest in your life.

A key purpose of the plateau is to hone your craft. The great gift of this wandering time is to perfect your purpose. Review your development so far. Go back to when you were just beginning this journey. Have you mastered the basic steps? What about the intermediate and advanced skills needed to implement your destiny? Have you integrated these different stages? Remember, it takes ten thousand hours of investment to come to a place of mastery. The spiritual plateau is the perfect place to fully develop what the Creator placed in your soul in the beginning.

As you cross the plateau, sometimes your progress will seem imperceptible and you will want to give up. When you want to throw in the towel, remember this jataka that the Buddha told of one of his previous incarnations:

Once there was a wealthy merchant crossing a great desert. The caravan ran out of water. The merchant ordered his servants to begin digging a well at the base of a green Yucca bush. They dug for days in the desert heat. Eventually they hit a huge rock and the servants stopped digging. In frustration they sat at the bottom of the hole cursing the merchant who stood above them. The merchant, with great gentleness, urged the men to keep striking the stone with their shovels. Repeatedly they did so, chipping away the rock. They became so exhausted that they stopped and wanted out of the hole. The merchant told them, "Why stop when you're so close!"

"Close? We're close to nothing!" exclaimed the servants. "The rock is solid way beyond this depth."

The merchant smiled and placed a mallet in a child's hand. The child was lowered into the well. The servants looked on in amazement as the merchant commanded the child to strike the rock. With one swing of his hammer, the child broke through and water began gushing into the hole. Upon finishing the story, the Buddha told his disciples that he was the merchant in a previous lifetime.[9]

If your plateau feels as futile as banging on a rock, picture the Buddha placing a hammer in your hand and become the child striking the stone. It may be that you are as close as one swing from the insight you need to propel you on your journey.

It may take months, even years, but something will spark and you will feel drawn to something new. Your steps will seem easier and your spirit lighter. You will gain momentum and soon you will be soaring again in a new direction.

Working without a Net

Alex is a very talented entrepreneur. For years he felt as though his life was on the Creator's trajectory. He knew in his heart that he had unleashed his purpose. Life changed when the economy soured. He had to file for bankruptcy, his house went into foreclosure, and he felt dumped on the curb. It took all the spiritual strength he could muster to stand back up and begin discovering what he was supposed to do next. However, the close relationship he felt with the Creator had almost vanished. He felt as if he was in a wasteland with no one to guide him. When Alex and I talked, I told him that he was on a plateau. Alex came to understand that he hadn't lost his faith, but that his faith was changing. It would take a few months, maybe even a few years, but I encouraged him to keep on walking and working, to find a mentor, and eventually he would climb to a higher place of life and spirituality.

Sure enough, after about a year, Alex felt a new sense of momentum. Passion began to rekindle in his soul as a new business opportunity began to develop. However, Alex still felt perplexed. While he felt confident that he was heading in the right direction, he no longer felt divine guidance. He described it as being on a high wire and working without a net. Before the economy tanked, he hadn't minded taking risks because he knew that if he fell, a divine hand was there to catch him. Now, he wasn't too sure. He wished the Creator was in front, guiding him. I explained to Alex that he was coming into the full understanding of what it meant to be sent!

When someone sends you on errand, you are given a direction and a purpose to fulfill, but the person who sends you can't go with you. He or she can't be there to tell you exactly what to do and how to do it, nor how to react to the challenges that you will face or the difficult people that you will confront. You are sent precisely because you have the right skills to fulfill this task. Your ability to intuit the right direction and when and where to ask for help is trusted. The person who sends you on this errand has faith in you. If your every move is scrutinized and corrected, initially you may appreciate the company, but eventually you feel stifled and resentful. You want the person to respect your talents and skills that empower you to fulfill the task on your own. This is how it is with the Creator.

You have been sent on your life journey because the Ultimate Being has faith in you. You were given gifts and sent on a trajectory. Yet you also have free will, a say-so with the expectation that you will "use it and choose it!" The very notion that you have been sent implies that you are going ahead of the Creator. You have been sent because your ability to choose, to react, to respond, to integrate, and to blaze a path in new directions is trusted by the One who created the cosmos.

The Tightrope Walker

There was a tightrope walker who stretched cables across vast chasms and walked with ease above the deep voids. He was unique because he always pushed a wheelbarrow.

One day he was set to walk across a canyon and a huge crowd gathered to watch him. There was tension in the air as the windy day caused the cable to bounce and slice the wind. Everyone held their breath as the man stood on the edge of the cliff, wheelbarrow in hand, pondering whether he should take the risk.

Many people were urging the man not to walk. However, there was one lone voice that shouted out, "Walk, I have faith in you!"

The tightrope walker turned his wheelbarrow toward the crowd to see who was urging him to take the risk. The man yelled again, "Walk, I have faith in you!"

The tightrope walker looked the man square in the eye and said, "I'll walk, if you ride!"

This is how it was when the Creator sent you. When you began life's journey you were safe on the side of the canyon. You had faith that you were protected from falling. As you grew and matured, your faith changed when you were challenged to step out from the safety of the cliff and ride in the divine wheelbarrow. It's a terrifying time when you are beckoned to put your faith on the line and allow the Creator to push you into new and different places.

Your faith changes yet again when you have crossed back and forth across the high wire and suddenly God vanishes. Now you are the one with the wheelbarrow on the edge of the cliff. Now you have to have faith in yourself. Or maybe, more important, you need to have faith in the One who has faith in you and has sent you to push the wheelbarrow. You need to take the courageous step and walk out across the chasm, knowing that you have all the skills and abilities that you need.

Your understanding of having faith and being sent changes yet again when you look down and find someone sitting in the wheelbarrow, gripping the sides in white-knuckled panic while looking back up at you. Because of some situation in life, that person has ended up in your wheelbarrow. You have been sent to carry the person across. His or her safety and fulfillment depend upon your ability to have faith in yourself and walk. If you are waiting for the Creator to comfort and guide you, then the person in your care suffers. You must step out, believe in yourself, and walk! The well-being of this person depends upon your action. The well-being of the entire world may depend on your ability to suck up the courage and walk across the chasm.

Lamed-Vovnik

There is a Jewish legend called the Lamed-Vovnik. Lamed-Vovnik is a combination of the Hebrew characters for the numbers three and six. According to the legend, in each generation HaShem sends thirty-six righteous people into the world. All of creation hinges on the actions of these thirty-six people. They are not presidents, heads of state, or military leaders. They are average folk who have no idea they are special. They might teach third grade, manage a sewage treatment plant, or be sitting in a jail cell. A Lamed-Vovnik might be a breast cancer patient or the person who welcomes you to Wal-Mart. If you were to ask them if they were special, they would look at you puzzled and say, "No." Yet, these are the people that HaShem has sent into the world to be special saviors. The world hangs on the thread of a Lamed-Vovnik's life.

What if you are a Lamed-Vovnik? What if you are the one the Creator has sent, and the entire civilization hangs in the balance of what you choose to do with your life? Suddenly channel surfing from one sitcom to another doesn't sound like such a good idea. The world needs you up and acting! You need to grab the wheelbarrow by both handles and charge across the tightrope. You need to engage your life and unleash divine potential!

You can dream about your purpose. You can see your destiny. You can feel in your bones what the Creator wants you to do. At some point, though, you have to go beyond dreaming and get going. You must suck up the courage, martial the commitment, align your relationships, and fly. It comes down to the courage and desire to fulfill your destiny. Do you have what it takes to dig down deep and cross a plateau? Do you have faith in yourself, not only to walk with a wheelbarrow across the chasm of life, but to walk it with someone who has faith in you? You must live as if you are the chosen, the special one, one who has been sent—a Lamed-Vovnik.

I have been sent to this world to wake you up to your purpose. But now it's in your hands. You now know the truth about your life. Before you were conceived, the Creator of the cosmos held your soul and planted a seed of destiny. You were hurled into the world to fulfill a great purpose. You have been sent here. The world needs what you have to offer. Engage your destiny. Join the seven billion other people in this world in creating something marvelous. Take the words that Jesus prayed to God, "As you have sent me into the world, so I have sent them into the world," straight from the Master's mouth. He has sent you. God has sent you. HaShem has sent you. Brahman has sent you. Allah has sent you. The Buddha has sent you. Now, go live your destiny.

Questions to Help You Discover and Explore Your Divine Purpose

1. It's time to be bold and clear. Finish this sentence: I have been sent into the world to . . .

2. If you are still cloudy on your divine purpose, make some guesses.

3. How has your divine destiny changed over the years?

4. Name the five people with whom you are going to share your divine purpose. What role do you want them to play in the development of your process?

5. What are the relationships that you need to untie yourself from so that you can begin fulfilling your destiny?

6. Maybe more than relationships, there are other issues from which you need to untie yourself. Are there addictions, memories, bad habits, others? List them. You will untie yourself from them only when you can name them.

7. Who are the negative people in your life that douse your dreams? How can their negativity be a positive force for compelling you forward?

8. When you were young, either as a child or an adolescent, who was it that doused your dreams and your confidence?

9. What does Jesus's teaching, "If you don't bring forth that which is within you, it will kill you" mean to you?

10. What is it within you that you need to bring forth? What are the thin things that fill your time? What are the priorities that you need to schedule? Make a list of the next ten steps that you have to take to begin fulfilling your destiny.

11. When was the last time you were on a spiritual plateau? What did it feel like? How long did it last? How did you finally break free from the plateau?

12. Maybe you're on a plateau right now. How long have you been on this plateau? How do feel about being there? What are the things that you have done that have helped move you across the plateau? Who have been the key people who have helped you across your plateau? What role have they played?

13. Have you felt God pouring an abundance of ideas and people over you? If so, how?

14. What will it take for you to engage God's dream for your life?

15. Who is in your wheelbarrow? Who is looking up to you to push them across the chasm?

16. Whom do you know who is Lamed-Vovnik?

17. Here is your final question. Describe your homecoming to heaven. You meet the Creator face-to-face. After welcoming you home the Ultimate Being asks you, "Well, did you fulfill your destiny?" How will you respond?

Acknowledgments

While I may have been the one to write this book, there are many people who truly became the authors. I want to give credit to some of those people who have been critical guides along the three-year journey it took to bring *Sent to Soar* to publication.

The people at Quest publishing have been inspirational to work with. Through her vision and expertise, Sharron Dorr, my managing editor, developed the full potential of *Sent to Soar*. My publicist, Jessica Salesek, used her skills in marketing to take *Sent to Soar* to people around the world. A huge thanks, also, to Martha Woolverton for her amazing gifts and her ability to fine-tune the details of the manuscript. Together, these three were a wonderful team. I was honored to work with them.

Matt Spruill has been my mentor through the whole process. Matt pushed, prodded, and goaded me to write this book. Matt sat with me as I outlined my chapters, edited my initial thoughts, and helped me overcome my own negative self-talk. If you have gotten anything from this book, it's Matt Spruill who gets the lion's share of the thanks.

For three years my colleague and great friend Mitch Samu challenged me to "stop messing around and get the book done!" His guidance, inspiration, and friendship have transformed my life. He helped me to believe not only in the book, but in myself. "Denver today, Sydney next year!"

ACKNOWLEDGMENTS

My good friend Kathy Brown was my editor. Kathy devoted hundreds of hours working through my drafts, deciphering my horrific spelling and typing errors. She worked with me page by page. Kathy . . . thank you, thank you, thank you. I hope to become the writer that you have shown me I can be. Garret Ray took my passive voice and made it come alive. Judy Buehrer helped the message of *Sent to Soar* flow from chapter to chapter. Thanks to all three of these wonderful folks for their commitment and professional insight.

There were several key people with whom I went public with and shared the early drafts of *Sent to Soar*. My good friend and life mentor John Rankin read the earliest version of the manuscript and provided key insights that guided my early thoughts. My good friends Rev. Don Shrumm and Rev. Mark Bigelow worked over the manuscript and guided the theology and writing style. Julie Pech did the same, and I changed many aspects of the book due to her insight.

Thanks also go to Coleen Hamph, whom I asked to read the manuscript from a non-Christian perspective. Her insights were invaluable.

I'd like to thank Bill Youmans for my author photograph, as well as helping me plumb the depths of the Buddha.

I want to thank my parents, George and Mary Benson, and my in-laws, Jean and Gene Brody, for their thoughtful readings. *Sent to Soar* took a major turn after Uncle Jim Peters read the manuscript, put it down, looked at me, and said, "Quit playing small." Thanks, Jim, for the shove.

I want to offer great thanks to the thousands of people over my thirty years of ministry who invited me to come into their lives and allowed me to help them discern their life direction.

If I have overlooked anyone, please know that from the bottom of my heart, I thank you all.

ACKNOWLEDGMENTS

My heart goes to my wife, Phoebe, and our three children. They stood beside me when I hit dead ends. Phoebe afforded me the time and space to write, leaving many home projects dangling like participles until the manuscript was finished. Phoebe gave her professional opinion on several chapters and listened quietly to others. She is my constant motivation to keep writing and sharing my ideas.

Notes

Unless otherwise noted, all biblical references are from the New Revised Standard Version.

Introduction

Epigraph: Eckhart Tolle, *A Guide to Enlightenment*.

My Story

Epigraph: Personal permission from the author, October 17, 2013.

Chapter One—The Goo That Is You

1. John 11:42 (my italics).

2. John 6:43 (Eugene H. Peterson, *The Message: The Bible in Contemporary Language*; my italics).

3. Galatians 1:1 (my italics).

4. Jeremiah 1:5.

5. John 17:18.

6. Romans 8:29.

7. Ephesians 1:4.

8. Psalm 139:16 (New American Standard Bible).

9. Jeremiah 1:5.

10. Rod Stryker, *The Four Desires: Creating a Life of Purpose, Happiness, Prosperity, and Freedom*, 18–21.

11. Kenneth Bowers, *God Speaks Again: An Introduction to the Baha'i Faith*.

12. John 9:3–5 (Peterson, *The Message*).

13. Galatians 1:1.

Chapter Two—The Dream Stream

1. Ephesians 3:20.

2. Leslie Dixon Weatherhead, *The Will of God*.

3. I Corinthians 15:54–55.

4. Genesis 39:2.

5. Genesis 39:21.

6. Genesis 45:5, 7 (my italics).

7. Vatsala Sperling, *Ganga: The River that Flows From Heaven to Earth*.

8. Psalm 138:8.

Chapter Three—The Holy Hairball

Epigraph: Coleman Barks, *The Essential Rumi*.

1. *Jatakas* are stories of the Buddha's previous incarnations.

2. Ken Kawasaki and Visakha Kawasaki, *Jataka Tales of the Buddha: An Anthology, Vol. II*.

3. Matthew 26:39.

4. Soorah al-Kahf (18): 29.

5. Jay McDaniel and Donna Bowman, eds., *Handbook of Process Theology*, 136.

6. I borrowed this term from Gregory Boyd's great book, *God of the Possibilities: A Biblical Introduction to the Open View of God*. Boyd does a wonderful job exploring the many ways that our free will is a critical aspect of God's creative process.

7. Tom Shadyac. *I Am.*

Chapter Four—The Divine Archer

Epigraph: Paulo Coelho. *The Way of the Bow*.

Chapter Five—The Divine Convergence

Epigraph: Coleman Barks, *The Soul of Rumi*.

1. Jack Hawley, *Reawakening the Spirit in Work*.

2. Ibid., 23, 24.

3. *Dojang* is the Korean term for the place where one practices Taekwondo.

4. John 15:11.

5. Eknath Easwaran, *The Unpanishads*.

6. Ibid., 255.

7. The Gandharvas were singers in the courts of the Gods; the Pitrs are the spirits of ancestors; the Devas are the deities; Indra is the God of war and the leader of the Devas; Virat is the knowledge of the universe; Prajapati is the God of procreation and protector of life.

8. Chakras are the energy centers in your body. The chakra over your heart is a powerful center of divine energy that flows through your body.

9. David Eagleman, *Sum: Forty Tales from the Afterlives*. I was intrigued with Eagleman's story, "Metamorphosis," where he presents the notion of the three deaths of our dying. I was particularly struck by the notion that our third death is the last time our name is mentioned on the planet. His ideas sparked my own creativity. I have taken the concept in a completely different direction for my own work.

10. You can begin the process of making your five wishes known by going to http://www.agingwithdignity.org.

11. Marsha Sinetar, *Do What You Love and the Money Will Follow*.

12. Matthew 19:24.

13. I Timothy 6:10.

14. I Corinthians 4:10.

15. Matthew 5:12.

16. Chris Holte, "Devadatta," accessed 3/25/2013, http://www.reocities.com/chris_holte/Buddhism/IssuesInBuddhism/devadatta.html.

17. John 6:66.

18. Stephen Mitchell, *Bhagavad Gita, A New Translation*, 194.

19. Mark 11:15–19, 27–33; Matthew 21:12–17, 23–27; Luke 19:45–48, 20:1–8; John 2:13–16.

20. Malcolm Gladwell, *Outliers: The Story of Success*.

21. http://www.tu.org.

Chapter Six—Sent to Suffer?

Epigraph: Helen Keller, *Optimism: An Essay*, Kindle EBook, loc. 38 of 385.

1. Nanomedicinecenter.com, accessed 10/18/2011, http://www.nanomedicinecenter.com.

2. Mama's Health, accessed 10/18/2011, http://www.mamashealth.com/heart_stat.asp.

3. Psalm 6:2–7.

4. Psalm 22:1.

5. Psalm 38:12.

6. Psalm 69:1–2.

7. Lamentations 3:1–3.

8. Lamentations 3:1–13.

9. Jeremiah 29:11.

10. Genesis 4.

11. Genesis 21:15–21.

12. Genesis 34.

13. 1 Samuel 31.

14. 2 Samuel 13.

15. 2 Samuel 11.

16. 2 Samuel 18.

17. 2 Kings 17.

18. 2 Kings 25.

19. Jeremiah 29:11.

20. Brian McKinlay, "Where is God when earthquakes kill?" January 15, 2010, accessed 10/19/2011, http://nottoomuch.com/archive/2010-m01.

21. Eknath Easwaran, trans., *The Unpanishads*, 160.

22. 1 John 4:8.

23. John 3:16.

24. Psalm 62:11.

25. Job 26:11.

26. Ephesians 1:19–23.

27. Psalm 46:1–7.

28. John 5:17.

29. 1 Corinthians 13:1.

30. John 17:18.

Chapter Seven—Sent as a Scourge?

Epigraph: Ursula Le Guin, *A Wizard of Earthsea*.

1. Rachel Lloyd, "Sex Trafficking," accessed 10/28/2013, http://www .halftheskymovement.org/issues/sex-trafficking.

2. Center for Victims of Torture, accessed 10/18/2011, http://www.cvt.org.

3. Scott Peck, *People of the Lie: The Hope for Healing Human Evil*.

4. Ibid., 42–43.

5. Iris Chang, *The Rape of Nanking*.

6. Immaculée Ilibagiza and Steve Erwin, *Left to Tell*.

7. Max Muller, trans., *The Dhammapada: The Buddha's Path of Truth*.

8. Deuteronomy 30:19.

9. Mitchell, *Bhagavad Gita*, 119.

10. 1 Thessalonians 5:15.

11. Eknath Easwaran, trans., *The Dhammapada*, 105.

12. Lewis Smedes, *The Art of Forgiving: When You Need to Forgive but Don't Know How*.

13. Jeremy Rifkin, *The Empathic Civilization: The Race to Global Consciousness in a World in Crisis*.

Chapter Eight—Sent Together

Epigraph: Richard H. Schmidt, *Prophet of Forgiveness: Desmond Tutu*.

1. Matthew 18:20.

2. Adherents.com, accessed 10/21/2011, http://www.adherents.com.

3. *Summum bonum* is Latin for the highest good.

4. Michael Battle, *Reconciliation: The Ubuntu Theology of Desmond Tutu*.

5. Ibid., 43.

6. Russell Matthew Linden, *Leading Across Boundaries: Creating Collaborative Agencies in a Networked World*.

7. Ibid., 171–72.

8. Ibid., 14, 77.

9. Corinthians 12:14–26.

10. Luke 20:16 (Peterson, *The Message*).

11. Linden, *Leading Across Boundaries*, 14.

12. Kawasaki and Kawasaki, *Jataka Tales, Vol. II*.

13. Linden, *Leading Across Boundaries*, 18.

14. Stephen Mitchell, trans., *Bhagavad Gita: A New Translation*, 54, 55.

15. Ibid., 65.

16. Laozi, *Tao Te Ching: A New English Version*, ch. 9.

17. Stephen Covey, *The Seven Habits of Highly Effective People*.

18. Acts 2:1–41.

19. Covey, *Seven Habits*, 277.

20. Linden, *Leading Across Boundaries*, 90, 190.

21. Ibid., 46.

22. Ibid.

23. John 15:13.

Chapter Nine—The Shootings

Epigraph: My wife, Phoebe Poos-Benson, on April 20, 1999, the day of the school shootings at Columbine.

1. Luke 23:34.

Chapter Ten—Sent to Soar!

Epigraph: William Hutchison Murray, "On Commitment and Hesitancy," in *The Scottish Himalayan Expedition*.

1. 2 Corinthians 1:20–22 (Peterson, *The Message*).

2. The quote is attributed to Ralph Waldo Emerson, though most scholars doubt he said this.

3. Luke 19:29–34.

4. Luke 4:28–30.

5. Matthew 5:11–12 (Peterson, *The Message*).

6. Gospel of Thomas, Line 70 (see the Gnostic Society Library, "The Nag Hammadi Library," accessed 11/18/2013, http://gnosis.org/naghamm/Pagels-Gnostic-Gospels.html).

7. Covey, *Seven Habits*, 145.

8. 2 Corinthians 2:12–17.

9. Kawasaki and Kawasaki, *Jataka Tales, Vol. II*, loc. 499 of 8954.

Bibliography

Barks, Coleman. *The Essential Rumi*. New York: Harper Collins, 2004.

———. *The Soul of Rumi*. New York: Harper One, 2001.

Battle, Michael. *Reconciliation: The Ubuntu Theology of Desmond Tutu*. Cleveland, OH: Pilgrim Press, 1997.

The Bible: New Revised Standard Version. Iowa Falls, IA: World, 1997.

Bowers, Kenneth. *God Speaks Again: An Introduction to the Baha'i Faith*. Wilmette: Baha'i, 2004.

Boyd, Gregory. *God of the Possibilities: A Biblical Introduction to the Open View of God*. Grand Rapids, MI: Baker Book House, 2000.

Chang, Iris. *The Rape of Nanking: The Forgotten Holocaust of World War II*. New York: Basic Books, 1997.

Cobb, John B., and David Ray Griffin. *Process Theology: An Introductory Exposition*. Philadelphia: Westminster, 1976.

Coelho, Paulo. *The Way of the Bow*. Barcelona: Sant Jordi Asociados, 2011.

BIBLIOGRAPHY

Cousins, Ewert H. *Process Theology: Basic Writings.* New York: Newman Press, 1971.

Covey, Stephen. *The Seven Habits of Highly Effective People: Powerful Lessons in Personal Change.* New York: Free Press, 1989.

Eagleman, David. *Sum: Forty Tales from the Afterlives.* New York: First Vintage Books.

Easwaran, Eknath, trans. *The Dhammapada.* Tomales, CA: Nilgiri Press, 2007.

————, trans. *The Unpanishads.* Tomales, CA: Nilgiri Press, 1987.

Friesen, Garry, and J. Robin Maxson. *Decision Making & the Will of God: A Biblical Alternative to the Traditional View.* Portland, OR: Multnomah Books, 1980.

Gladwell, Malcolm. *Outliers: The Story of Success.* New York: Little, Brown, 2008.

Hawley, Jack. *Reawakening the Spirit in Work.* San Francisco: Berrett-Koehler, 1993.

Ilibagiza, Immaculée, and Steve Erwin. *Left to Tell: Discovering God amidst the Rwandan Holocaust.* Carlsbad, CA: Hay House, 2006.

Kawasaki, Ken, and Visakha Kawasaki. *Jataka Tales of the Buddha: An Anthology, Vol. II.* http://www.brelief.org, 2011.

Keller, Helen. *Optimism: An Essay.* Boston: Merrymount Press. Kindle EBook.

Kellerman, Jonathan. *Savage Spawn: Reflections on Violent Children*. New York: Ballantine, 1999.

Laozi. *Tao Te Ching: A New English Version*. Translated by Stephen Mitchell. New York: Harper & Row, 1988.

Le Guin, Ursula. *A Wizard of Earthsea*. New York: Bantam Dell.

Linden, Russell Matthew. *Leading across Boundaries: Creating Collaborative Agencies in a Networked World*. San Francisco: Jossey-Bass, 2010.

McDaniel, Jay B., and Donna Bowman. *Handbook of Process Theology*. St. Louis, MO: Chalice Press, 2006.

Mitchell, Stephen, trans. *Bhagavad Gita: A New Translation*. New York: Harmony, 2000.

Muller, Max, trans. *The Dhammapada: The Buddha's Path of Truth*. Kindle EBook.

Murray, William Hutchison. *The Scottish Himalayan Expedition*. London: J. M. Dent, 1951.

Peck, M. Scott. *People of the Lie: The Hope for Healing Human Evil*. New York: Simon and Schuster, 1983.

Peterson, Eugene H. *The Message: The Bible in Contemporary Language*. Colorado Springs: NavPress, 2002.

Rifkin, Jeremy. *The Empathic Civilization: The Race to Global Consciousness in a World in Crisis*. New York: Penguin Group, 2009.

BIBLIOGRAPHY

Schmidt Richard H. *Prophet of Forgiveness: Desmond Tutu*. Cincinnati, OH: Forward Movement, 2004.

Shadyac, Tom. *I Am*. Universal City, CA: Shady Acres, 2011. CD.

Sinetar, Marsha. *Do What You Love, the Money Will Follow: Discovering Your Right Livelihood*. New York: Dell, 1989.

Smedes, Lewis B. *The Art of Forgiving: When You Need to Forgive and Don't Know How*. Nashville: Moorings, 1996.

Sperling, Vatsala. *Ganga: The River that Flows from Heaven to Earth*. Rochester, VT: Bear Cub Books, 2008.

Stryker, Rod. *The Four Desires: Creating a Life of Purpose, Happiness, Prosperity, and Freedom*. New York: Delacort Press, 2011.

Stumpf, Samuel Enoch. *Socrates to Sartre: A History of Philosophy*. New York: McGraw-Hill, 1975.

Titus, Harold H., and Marilyn S. Smith. *Living Issues in Philosophy*. New York: D. Van Nostrand, 1974.

Tolle, Eckhart. *A Guide to Enlightenment*. Novato, CA: New World Library, 1997.

Towey, Jim. *Aging with Dignity: The Five Wishes*. Tallahassee, FL: Aging With Dignity, 2011. http://www.agingwithdignity.org.

Weatherhead, Leslie Dixon. *The Will of God*. New York: Abingdon-Cokesbury, 1944.

Index

pantheon of gods and, 10
planting dharma within, 73
union with, 76, 80
brains, mirror neurons in, 157–60
Buddha
    balancing insight and action, 52
    on breakthroughs, 227–28
    on evil, 148
    on free will, 51–52
    on hatred and love, 154
    on hoarding, 173–74
    on integration of spirituality and
        life, 175
    persecution of, 91
    on suffering, 130
Buddhism
    choice in, 26
    guiding principles of, 26–27
    intentional practices in, 52,
        137
    tonglen and, 137
"But-But" game, 183–84

C
Cain and Abel, 53
Center for Victims of Torture, 142
chakras, 77
Chang, Iris, 146–47
childhood, 37
children, empowering dreams of,
    221–22
choices. *See also* free will
    at Columbine High School, 196
    Columbine shootings and, 206
    daily challanges of, 151–52

evil and, 144–45
forgiveness as, 155
in Jewish scriptures, 52–54,
    124–25
preparation for, 134
response of Creator to, 69
Christianity
    anger and, 77
    denominations of, 165
    guiding principles of, 23–24
    love in, 126
    suffering and, 125
churches, turf wars in, 170
circumstantial will, 35–39, 44,
    67–68, 133
clarity, 213–15
co-creators, 57
Coelho, Paul, 62
coincidences, 39
collaboration
    after Columbine shootings, 199
    Christian disciples and, 164–65
    Creator's presence in, 166–67
    ego impeding, 168–70
    turf wars and, 170
    Western culture and, 167
colt (analogy), 217
Columbine Community Library,
    195, 196
Columbine High School shootings,
    188
    bringing order after, 196–202
    challenges and questions
        following, 205–10
    choosing to act after, 191–93

MORE PRAISE FOR STEPHEN POOS-BENSON'S
SENT TO SOAR

"This book is a great illustration of the human inclination toward unity among diversity for the good of one and all."

—**Kailash Chandra Upadhyay**, Head Priest, Hindu Temple and Cultural Center of the Rockies, Littleton, CO

"I had been a member of Rev. Poos-Benson's Columbine United Church for six years before the Columbine shootings. Immediately after the tragedy Steve, his congregation, and our nearby rehabilitation hospital became close partners. Together, we established a temporary crisis center at Craig, and for months we worked to heal the catastrophically injured and their families and ourselves at the same time. *Sent to Soar* is an insightful and helpful book. I highly recommend it."

—**Kenny Hosack,** M.A., Craig Hospital

"In a world of lost souls looking for some purpose beyond earning a few more dollars, *Sent to Soar* invites us to claim a larger perspective: life isn't just about 'me'; it's about *us*. Steve gives us a wakeup call that encompasses the world's great religions to get us in touch with deep possibilities waiting to be unleashed. Read this compelling book and expect transformation."

—**Jim Symons,** CEO of Towards a Millennium of Compassion

"In the summer that my surgeon said that 'this is my life's work' prior to removing my brain tumor, I read *Sent to Soar*. This book rekindled my belief in a purpose-driven life. Steve's empathetic and knowledgeable reading of multiple faith traditions combine with decades of pastoral experience to give substance to his challenges to the reader. The book deepened my insight into my own faith tradition while strengthening my knowledge of connections to other faith traditions."

—**Dr. Mike Charles**, Professor, College of Education, Pacific University